MIDNIGHT IN LONDON

MIDNIGHT IN LONDON

The Anglo-Irish Treaty Crisis 1921

Colum Kenny

EASTWOOD BOOKS

First published 2021 by Eastwood Books
Dublin, Ireland
www.eastwoodbooks.com
www.wordwellbooks.com

Eastwood Books is an imprint of the Wordwell Group

Eastwood Books
The Wordwell Group
Unit 9, 78 Furze Road
Sandyford
Dublin, Ireland

© Colum Kenny, 2021

ISBN: 978-1-913934-19-4 (Paperback)
ISBN: 978-1-913934-27-9 (Ebook)

British Library Cataloguing in Publication Data.
A catalogue record for this book is available from the National Library of
Ireland and the British Library.

Front cover image: Arthur Griffith and Michael Collins leaving 10 Downing
Street in 1921. *Courtesy National Library of Ireland [NPA MKN33]*

Typesetting and design by the Wordwell Group
Copyediting by Myles McCionnaith
Printed in the EU

'We made a compromise;
no compromise is logically defensible.'

Prime Minister Lloyd George to Michael Collins, 1921.

CONTENTS

Preface

I n the middle of the night of 5–6 December 1921, shortly after two o'clock in London, Irish and British negotiators signed an agreement for a treaty that would end the Irish War of Independence and create an independent Irish state. This is the story of that fraught night and of the crisis that surrounded it.

Just hours before the Irish signed, Prime Minister Lloyd George had confronted them across the table and delivered what Winston Churchill termed 'an ultimatum'. The Irish must accept the agreement as it stood then, after nearly two months of wrangling in London, or else face an immediate and determined resumption of war.

The British negotiators, members of a government that had sent the despised Black and Tans and Auxiliaries to fight in Ireland, waited at 10 Downing Street while the Irish left for their rented house in Hans Place to consider the ultimatum. Arthur Griffith, Minister for Foreign Affairs, chaired the Irish side.

Éamon de Valera, the Irish premier (or 'president', as the senior minister in the Irish revolutionary government was termed), had refused to go to London for the substantial negotiations.

The Irish did not know if the ultimatum was real or a bluff. But their two senior delegates, Arthur Griffith and Michael Collins, believed that they had already achieved enough to sign an agreement that night. They thought that the deal would allow the new Irish Free State to work towards the goal of a fully independent and united Ireland. In the end, all five delegates decided to sign the agreement rather than risk war. Although that agreement has frequently been described informally as 'The Treaty', there was no treaty in law unless and until the agreement was ratified by Dáil Éireann and by the parliament at Westminster.

As Éamon de Valera ('Dev') said on 14 December 1921, when members of the Dáil began their debate on the Treaty, 'The main point is settled. By the admission of the delegates themselves, and it is the only thing we are concerned with here, we did not send them, and it would be ridiculous to think that we could send five men to complete a treaty without the right of ratification by this assembly. That is the only thing that matters. Therefore it is agreed that this Treaty is simply an agreement and that it is not binding until the Dáil ratifies it.'

The terms agreed at 10 Downing Street during the night of 5–6 December were recommended to Dáil Éireann by a majority of the seven members of the Irish Cabinet, and ratified by a majority of the Dáil on 7 January 1922. Each Sinn Féin TD (*Teachta Dála*: Dáil deputy) had been elected on a platform that committed him or her to the Irish Republic that had been declared by rebels during the 1916 Rising. Most agreed with Griffith and Collins that the Treaty was a stepping-stone to greater independence. Those who chose to oppose the Treaty militarily during 1922 lost a destructive civil war that poisoned Irish politics for more than a generation, hardened the border and set back the new state. Whether or not that civil war was avoidable is a question beyond the scope of the present book.

In writing this account, the author has relied largely on national archives and other official public records in Britain and Ireland – many of which are now readily available online – and on first-hand accounts such as those recorded decades later by the Irish Bureau of Military History. These are lively but at times poignant. The temptation to speculate about 'what might have been' and to jump to conclusions based only on partial evidence (often 'partial' in both senses of that word) can be almost irresistible. The absence of minutes or detailed notes of many meetings of the Peace Conference (as the Treaty negotiations were sometimes known) and its sub-conferences is frustrating. Certain personal papers once cited by some writers have vanished or are otherwise unavailable now. The fact that Griffith and Collins died within nine months of that night in London meant that they left no later memoir.

Among helpful published sources are the *Whitehall Diary* of UK Cabinet Secretary Thomas Jones (3 vols, Oxford University Press, 1971, out of print), the official reports of public and private Dáil debates that are now also available online, and the multivolume *Documents on Irish Foreign Policy* (ed. Michael Kennedy *et al.*; Royal Irish Academy, 1998–2020) which guides one to particular records in the National Archives that are now too, in many cases, also online. I am grateful for the stimulation of various biographies of leading players in this drama, and to Brian Maye in particular for information about his correspondence with Thomas Pakenham. I wish to thank also the librarians or keepers of the National Library of Ireland, the Royal Irish

Academy, Bray Public Library, Dublin City University, King's Inns, the National Archives of Ireland, the National Archives of the United Kingdom, UCD Archives, Trinity College Dublin and the University of Birmingham. I am also grateful to the Capuchin Order and to the Parliamentary Archives, Houses of Parliament, Westminster. Ronan Colgan and others at Eastwood Books have been enthusiastic throughout. My wife Catherine Curran has been patient and supportive, and my sons inspiring.

Authors have their own opinions, and it is good to be frank about them. I believe that, given the circumstances in which they found themselves, the Irish delegates were right to sign an agreement for a treaty, particularly as it still required the approval of Dáil Éireann. It would have been an irresponsible gamble for them to take a chance on the British ultimatum being a bluff. If it were not, then Lloyd George would have ended the talks and resumed a war of which the Irish were already weary and which Sinn Féin might not win.

The chairmen of the two delegations, Griffith and Lloyd George, had a particular burden to carry. They were there to make a deal for their peoples – to avoid further deaths, if reasonably possible. No deal is done without some compromise. The British brought things to a head with their ultimatum on the night of 5–6 December, but the Irish for their part had also held out the threat of a renewed War of Independence.

In telling the story of that dramatic night in London, I have assumed that all parties to the dispute – Irish and British, whatever their political perspectives – were sincere and acted in good faith – if not always wisely. Their dilemma was as much political and pragmatic as it was one of moral principle. The night of 5–6 December 1921 was a crucial turning point in Irish history.

MERRY LAUGHTER

Their 'talk was of the merriest', wrote one of them, and the room at 10 Downing Street 'rang with laughter'. It was two hours to midnight and four of the most powerful politicians in the British Empire were waiting for three Irishmen to return. Two miles away, at their rented London house in Knightsbridge, the Irish were not laughing.

Austen Chamberlain was one of those in Downing Street. He fiddled with his monocle while time passed. Years later, recalling those hours, he was to describe the mood of British ministers on the night of 5–6 December 1921 as 'a problem for the psychologist'. The day had been one of unrelieved mental and emotional strain, being locked in difficult talks with three of the five Irish negotiators in London. According to Chamberlain, 'The tension reached its height during the long wait for the return of the Irish delegates in the evening. Peace or war – the issue still hung in the balance.' While waiting, Prime Minister David Lloyd George managed to sleep for twenty-five minutes. He had been up working since five in the morning.

Chamberlain was leader of the Conservative and Unionist Party in the House of Commons; his was the larger party in a coalition government with Lloyd George's Liberals. He wrote in his memoir *Down the Years* (Cassell, 1935), 'There is a limit to human endurance.' He regarded the laughter as a British reaction to the tension. Perhaps it was. Or maybe these men sensed victory. They had given the Irish an ultimatum to sign an agreement or face an immediate renewal of the War of Independence. Had the men in Downing Street, pillars of British imperialism, really reached the limits of human endurance after two months? Or had they simply run out of patience with the printer/journalist, the office clerk, the two lawyers and the agriculturalist who had tied them up in talks since early October. Did the Irish so easily exhaust David Lloyd George, Austen Chamberlain, Colonial Secretary Winston Churchill and Lord Chancellor Birkenhead?

We do not know if the British smoked as they waited, if Winston Churchill lit up one of those fat cigars that later became so associated with him when prime minister during the Second World War. We do know that, when it came to endurance, the British Empire itself had considerable experience in testing it. Joseph Chamberlain, Austen's father and the Liberal Unionist Secretary of the Colonies from 1895 to 1903, had helped to manage the British adventure in South Africa that was the Boer War. Joseph remained (as the Oxford *Dictionary of National Biography* puts it) 'ready to do what he could by rough means as well as fair to strengthen the imperial power' in South Africa. Winston Churchill had served in Egypt and was fully aware of the slaughter near Omdurman in the Sudan in 1898, when the

British used machine guns to kill ten thousand desert tribesmen while losing fewer than fifty members of their army that same day. Lloyd George had been prime minister for more than two years when, on 13 April 1919, Colonel Reginald Edward Dyer was responsible for the British Indian Army attacking a peaceful protest at Jallianwala Bagh in Amritsar, Punjab, killing about four hundred people and injuring more than one thousand. F.E. Smith, before becoming Lord Chancellor, had earned himself a reputation as Edward Carson's 'galloper' at the torchlight processions and parades of armed unionist Volunteers in Ulster. He had subsequently led the prosecution of Roger Casement, who attempted to arm the nationalist Volunteers of southern Ireland.

Anguish in Knightsbridge

On 19 December 1921, addressing his fellow deputies in Dáil Éireann, Robert Barton recalled himself and Arthur Griffith and Michael Collins arriving for the final session of talks at 10 Downing Street earlier that month, 'In the struggle that ensued Arthur Griffith sought, repeatedly, to have the decision between war and peace on the terms of the Treaty referred back to this assembly [Dáil Éireann]. This proposal Mr. Lloyd George directly negatived. He claimed that we were plenipotentiaries and that we must either accept or reject.'

According to Barton, the English prime minister, 'with all the solemnity and the power of conviction that he alone, of all men I have met, can impart by word and gesture – the vehicles by which the mind of one man oppresses and impresses the mind of another – declared that the signature and recommendation of every member of our delegation was necessary or war would follow immediately. He gave us until 10 o'clock [that night] to make up our minds, and it was then about 8.30.'

Griffith, Collins and himself had immediately left Downing Street for their headquarters at Hans Place. Not all five Irish delegates attended every session of the talks, and on this occasion their colleagues George Gavan Duffy and Éamonn Duggan were waiting for them there. Barton told Dáil Éireann on 19 December 1921, 'We returned to our house to decide upon our answer. The issue before us was whether we should stand behind our proposals for external association [Ireland outside the Empire but in a new form of relationship with it], face war and maintain the Republic, or whether we should accept inclusion in the British Empire and take peace. Arthur Griffith, Michael Collins, and Éamonn Duggan were for acceptance and peace; Gavan Duffy and myself were for refusal – war or no war.'

They all had to decide that night whether to sign the agreement for a treaty as then drafted or possibly face renewed war. Barton was to tell the Dáil, 'An answer that was not unanimous committed you to immediate war, and the responsibility for that was to rest directly upon those two delegates who refused to sign. For myself, I preferred war. I told my colleagues so, but for the nation, without consultation, I dared not accept that responsibility. The alternative which I sought to avoid seemed to me a lesser outrage than the violation of what is my faith.' Turning to de Valera that day in the Dáil, Barton added that he had not been prepared to decide whether to commit his nation to immediate war, 'without you, Mr. President, or the Members of the Dáil, or the nation having an opportunity to examine the terms upon which war could be avoided.' He had earlier pleaded with de Valera to come to London.

On 21 December 1921 Barton's fellow delegate Gavan Duffy told deputies:

Our delegates returned to us to inform us that four times they had all but broken and that the fate of Ireland must be decided that night. Lloyd George had issued to them an ultimatum to this effect: 'It must now be peace or war. My messenger goes tonight to Belfast. I have here two answers, one enclosing the Treaty, the other declaring a rupture, and, if it be a rupture, you shall have immediate war, and the only way to avert that immediate war is to bring me the undertaking to sign of every one of the plenipotentiaries, with a further undertaking to recommend the Treaty to Dáil Éireann and to bring me that by 10 o'clock. Take your choice.' I shall not forget the anguish of that night, torn as one was between conflicting duties.

Gavan Duffy conceded that the ultimatum may have been a bluff, but he thought that 'every one of those who had heard the British Prime Minister believed beyond all reasonable doubt that this time he was not play acting, and that he meant what he said.'

Gavan Duffy also quoted from what he dubbed 'the semi-official organ of Mr. Lloyd George – the *Daily Chronicle*', which he said reported next day that 'Before the delegates separated for dinner the Prime Minister made his final appeal. He made it clear that the draft before them was the last concession which any British Government could make. The issue now was the grim choice between acceptance and immediate war.' Such publicity meant that the prime minister would lose face with his party and electorate if it transpired that he was bluffing. At Hans Place, said Gavan Duffy, 'we had to make this choice within three hours and to make it without any reference to our Cabinet, to our Parliament or to our people. And that monstrous iniquity was perpetrated by the man who had invited us under his roof in order, moryah [Irish: *mar dhea*, 'as if'], to make a friendly settlement.'

As the British ministers waited for the Irish to return, and Downing Street rang with their laughter, the hands of the clock moved towards midnight. The Peace Conference had adjourned just after eight o'clock that evening. Lloyd George wanted talks to resume at ten o'clock, but the Irish at Hans Place struggled with the British ultimatum. UK Cabinet Secretary Thomas Jones is said to have phoned Hans Place several times to enquire about progress.

Arthur Griffith, chairman of the Irish delegation, wrote a short contemporary account of events on that night. His fellow delegate Robert Barton composed a somewhat longer one the next day for Éamon de Valera in Ireland, at Griffith's request. Their accounts shed little light on what happened as the Irish considered the ultimatum. More than three decades later, Barton was to claim that 'for three hours we had a most frightful battle in the delegation, among ourselves, at which the most terrific things were said to Gavan Duffy and to me by Collins and Griffith and Duggan.' But in his contemporary note, written for de Valera, he stated simply, 'There was a discussion amongst ourselves lasting from 9 [p.m.] to 11.15 at 22 Hans Place, at which a decision was eventually reached to recommend the Treaty to the Dáil. At 11.30 [p.m.] we returned to Downing Street and attacked the document again.'

What Kathleen Saw

At about half past eight in the evening on 5 December, Griffith's personal secretary, Kathleen McKenna, heard cars pull up outside. She and other Irish back-up staff and some advisors were waiting in the delegation's two rented houses. These were close to one another, at 22 Hans Place and 15 Cadogan Gardens. The *Capuchin Annual* of 1971 contains her account of what happened next.

McKenna wrote that Collins, followed by members of his small Irish security detail, rushed through the hall of the house at Cadogan Gardens and dashed upstairs. After a short time Eamon ('Ned') Broy came pounding down to her office and said he would go with her over to Hans Place, where she might be needed. Broy, a former member of the Dublin Metropolitan Police, had once smuggled Michael Collins into the headquarters of its intelligence-gathering G Division to trawl through files. He would later serve as Commissioner of the Garda Síochána, the police force of the Irish state. In London, he was acting as

Collins's private secretary and bodyguard. On the opening day of the Peace Conference, some pressmen saw, or thought they saw, the outline of revolvers in the pockets of Broy and other Irishmen who accompanied the Irish delegation in Rolls Royce cars to Downing Street. Broy now escorted McKenna over to Hans Place, 'It was a pleasant, calm, pitch dark, foggy night [...] Conversing in low tones and walking on the road, we were conscious that figures were loitering everywhere in the shadows. From a kind of shop-window arcaded place three or four of them stepped out unexpectedly before us and without uttering a syllable blocked us. One flashed an electric torch in Broy's face and by its light I saw they had pistols. They scrutinised Broy thoroughly, passing the torch over his head, face and body, then silently slunk away.'

McKenna's father, William Kenna, was one of a circle of Irish culture enthusiasts in Co. Meath who, in 1902, had briefly produced *Sinn Féin–Oldcastle Monthly Review*. Its title involved one of the nationalist uses of the Irish words *sinn féin*, meaning 'we ourselves', that preceded Griffith's adoption of those two words as the name of his political movement from 1905. Griffith used to visit her family home regularly. Patrick Maume notes in the *Dictionary of Irish Biography* that she and her siblings, when teenagers, added the Irish prefix 'Mc' to their family name. This was an indication of their nationalist sentiments.

Lloyd George had wanted the Irish delegates to return to Downing Street by ten o'clock, but Kathleen found Hans Place quiet, 'Apart from the clicking of typewriters the house was silent, almost tense, as if it, too, felt the gravity of the impending events.' Collins himself then came over from Cadogan Gardens, saying that the vicinity was bristling with Scotland Yard men, 'He was impatient to find that the others were not already down in the hall. He stalked nervously up and down the dining room, then went to the end of it where there was a kind of buffet. Tom poured out a sherry for him. Mick drank very little, but when he did he preferred sherry.'

Upstairs, Gavan Duffy and Duggan were considering the ultimatum issued by Lloyd George. Kathleen wrote that Collins did not go upstairs, 'Instead he stalked, like a wild beast in a cage, up and down the room, morose, silent and sullen, then plumped down on an ordinary dining-room chair (not an arm-chair) that happened to be in the centre of the room in exact line with that part of the stairs down which those who were to join him would have to come. With his attaché case, and thrown over it his old grey-brown dust-coat, hanging down in one hand and almost touching the carpet, and his other hand holding on his knee his felt hat, he fell into a profound sleep. Poor "big fellah!"'

Collins had an effect on women, 'As I gazed at him my heart ached with anguish at the thought of what this man's mental torture must be. I realised fully all the weight of responsibility placed by events beyond his control upon his young, generous shoulders. With the tenderness with which a mother watches her fever-stricken child I gazed upon his pale face, now relaxed and calm, and wanted to push away the rebellious lock hanging on his forehead. In the depths of my soul – in one of those places "never sounded or known" – I preserve an image of that scene which none save myself witnessed that night of 5 December, 1921.'

With people tired and emotional in 1921, their memories of events were sometimes to differ considerably. In the *Capuchin Annual* in 1971, Kathleen McKenna disagreed indirectly with Barton, who, in 1954, had told the Bureau of Military History that Collins was wrangling and arguing upstairs. She wrote, 'I want to say that it is as true as death that Michael Collins's decision to sign, as well as Arthur Griffith's, had been irrevocably taken when they left Downing Street late that same evening and that not only had he no discussion with those in Griffith's room and in [Erskine] Childers's office but he did not even put one step forward to go upstairs. What the others were doing is another tale; the upshot of their discussions was that first Duggan, then Barton and finally Gavan Duffy decided to sign.'

Kathleen remembered the men upstairs coming down 'solemnly' and, along with Collins and the Irish security detail, taking their places in the waiting cars to return to Downing Street, 'All anxiety, I stood seeing them off [...] It was almost midnight.' As they arrived at Downing Street, reported the Press Association next day, 'it was noticed that they looked grave and stern. They had neither word not smile for those that crowded round.'

Bursting to Fragments

At the very first session of peace talks on 11 October 1921, Lloyd George said that he understood it was the wish of the Irish to have no notes taken. The British had no objection to a verbatim shorthand record or a stenographer, but there had been no transcription of the meetings between de Valera and Lloyd George in July 1921 and the Irish again chose to let the talks flow without a formal record of them.

Nevertheless, Griffith kept de Valera informed by letter throughout the two months, and even on 6 December sent him what he called 'the barest outline' of the final, difficult meeting that had just ended. He wrote, 'This is a very hasty and imperfect sketch of what happened in a prolonged conference on four occasions during which it was on the point of bursting to fragments.' He stated, 'Things were so strenuous and exhausting that the sequence of conversation is not in many cases clear in my mind today.' He added that he had asked Barton to make 'a long Memo. of events', which they would now bring back to

Dublin. Barton's memorandum is in fact not particularly 'long' given the length of the meeting, and it is frustratingly vague in ways that will be identified later.

It is clear from Griffith's own account how difficult he had found the meeting of 5–6 December, 'We were there all day and probably half the night – with a couple of breaks.' He told de Valera, 'The Conference opened with the British Delegates in a bad mood. They had a full Cabinet meeting previously and apparently had had a rough time.'

According to Griffith, 'Lloyd George began by suggesting we had let him down over the Ulster proposals. We denied this and argued we must have a reply from Craig [Prime Minister of Northern Ireland] refusing or accepting these proposals before we proceeded. The others pointed out that as they were prepared to go ahead with their proposals irrespective of Craig there was no ground for our contention.' The British had ostensibly put pressure on the unionists to come into a united Ireland of some kind, within the British Empire, or else face a redrawing of the new border established by the British in 1920. Griffith consistently pressed for clarity and commitment on that option before making a final decision on an agreement for a treaty.

Griffith told de Valera on 6 December that 'We went on this line of argument for a while when Lloyd George declared we were trying to bring about a break on Ulster. The question was, would we or would we not come within the community of nations known as the British Empire. The question must be answered because it was the question of peace or war.' Griffith wrote that he was 'determined not to let them break on the Crown' – in other words, not to give the British an excuse to blame the Irish for too bluntly or unreasonably refusing to remain a member of the Empire – which might appear internationally to be an extreme position to take.

The British had insisted since the truce in July 1921 that a new Irish state could not become a full republic having no link to the Crown. Indeed, without such a link, all-Ireland unity was even more unlikely than otherwise. Griffith responded to Lloyd George, 'I said, provided we came to agreement on other points, I would accept inclusion in the Empire on the basis of the Free State. After that they went on and gave way on fiscal autonomy wholly, yielded more on defence and some minor matters. Then they asked me whether I spoke for myself or for the delegation. I said I spoke for myself. Then they said they were standing together as a unit. We should do the same.'

Griffith, in his note written on 6 December 1921, refers to the British ultimatum simply as 'the question of peace or war'. He glosses over the delegates' return to Hans Place during the adjournment, 'Later on we met again. We had discussed the matter and decided our course.'

After going back to Downing Street as midnight approached, the Irish proposed some amendments to the draft agreement, 'They accepted most of them when we said we spoke as a united delegation, that we were willing to recommend inclusion with the other states in the Empire [*i.e.* in the Commonwealth]. It was on this basis, by the way, that they altered the oath of allegiance – earlier in the day. At 2.12 a.m. we signed the document.'*

*Griffith to de Valera, 'Conference on Ireland: Mr Griffith's notes of two sub-conferences held on December 5th/December 6th 1921, at 10 Downing Street, No. 1 at 3 p.m., No. 2 at 11.30 p.m. to 2.30 a.m., Irish National Archives, DE 2/304/5/6, not published in *Documents on Irish Foreign Policy*.

SHAKING HANDS

In 1935 Austen Chamberlain was to write that the British and Irish delegates never shook hands until their negotiations ended in agreement. He was mistaken in respect to the prime minister. For at the opening session of the Peace Conference on 11 October 1921, Lloyd George stood by the door of the meeting room to greet the Irishmen. The other British, however, were already in their places behind the large conference table, thus avoiding close personal contact.

Like politicians anywhere, the British and Irish were conscious of how their encounters with an enemy might look to their backbenchers and constituents. Having spent much of the previous two years dismissing Sinn Féin as murderers, despite that party's widespread electoral support, and having long tried to arrest or kill its members, the UK government was not about to appear enthusiastic about being in the same room and talking terms with that party's representatives. For their part, Griffith, Collins and Barton were acutely conscious of the fact that two of the seven Irish Cabinet members, Cathal Brugha and Austin Stack back in Dublin, were hostile to the entire process.

In his account of the full Treaty negotiations, *Peace by Ordeal* (Cape, 1935), Frank Pakenham thought that 'It was very doubtful whether the Irish delegates would consent to shake hands with Sir Hamar Greenwood, Chief Secretary for Ireland, on whom the publics of both countries were agreed in fixing official responsibility for the Black-and-Tans' – that special Crown force unleashed by London during the Irish War of Independence.

Simply walking through the door of Downing Street gave the Irish representatives a certain standing that was difficult for some British politicians to take. At the unique Cabinet meeting that Lloyd George had convened in Scotland in September 1921 to discuss letters then being exchanged between the prime minister and de Valera, UK Cabinet Secretary Thomas Jones made a note in his diary of Chamberlain saying, 'We cannot continue a correspondence of this kind indefinitely. We lose caste.' His use of the Indian concept of caste, signifying for the clubbable British ministers a potentially diminished status, implicitly categorised the Irish as an inferior or subject people. In a useful overview of British political attitudes towards the eventual Treaty agreement, Seán Donnelly has pointed out that 'by recognising the legitimacy of Irish national aspirations and repudiating historic claims to racial and civilisational superiority, the Treaty was felt by many to run counter to the course of British history and consequently struck at the very heart of the British sense of self' (*Irish Studies Review*, no. 27 [4], 2019). It was by no means only on one side of the Irish Sea that some found any compromise difficult.

The Irish delegation – accompanied by Art O'Brien, who was the revolutionary Irish Republic's representative in London – arrived a few minutes before the appointed hour of eleven o'clock for the first meeting on 11 October. They were shown into the office of Sir Philip Sassoon, a British MP for Hythe in Kent and a parliamentary private secretary to Lloyd George. O'Brien asked to come into the conference room to be introduced to the British delegation, in order, in turn, to introduce his countrymen to the British. Cabinet Secretary Thomas Jones accompanied O'Brien along the passage; next in line was Arthur Griffith (as Irish chairman), then Collins, followed by the other Irish delegates. After de Valera, Griffith – as Minister for Foreign Affairs – was the most senior member of the Irish Cabinet. Lloyd George met each man at the door of the conference room, shaking his hand before directing him to his place along one side of the table opposite the British representatives. Lloyd George then identified his own colleagues, without further handshakes.

The British diplomatically ensured that no Irishman was placed opposite Sir Hamar Greenwood, who was seen by many in Ireland as 'coercion incarnate' (as a Dublin Castle official put it).

Almost a full two months of negotiations followed. They ended with the agreement for a treaty being signed on the night of 5–6 December. One of those present then, Austen Chamberlain, later wrote that British ministers 'moved down our side of the table as the Irish representatives rose to leave, and shook hands with them for the first time'. There appears to be no photograph of any member of one team with a member of the other team, and the final signing was not a celebrated public event. Negotiators on both sides had their domestic detractors. Unlike the Treaty of Versailles, between Allied powers and the defeated Germans in 1919, the Anglo-Irish deal was clearly a compromise rather than an outright victory for either side.

PRESIDENT AND PRINCE

Missing from the Irish team in Downing Street was a key player. Éamon de Valera stayed in Ireland for the duration of the Peace Conference. In July 1921, when de Valera went to London just days after a truce in the War of Independence was agreed, he had met Prime Minister Lloyd George four times. Lloyd George now returned to the table from October to December, alongside his own most senior ministers.

Some saw a peace conference without de Valera as akin to the proverbial performance of Shakespeare's *Hamlet* without the prince, that play's main character. Others have referenced Machiavelli's *The Prince*, a notorious treatise on cunning statecraft. De Valera gave two pieces of advice to a young Richard Mulcahy about politics, 'study economics and read *The Prince*.' De Valera carried a copy of the book with him in America and noted its neat turn of phrase. His absence from London meant that Irish delegates there continually tried to interpret his thinking. They made tiring journeys overland and over sea to brief him, particularly for a draining Cabinet meeting in Dublin two days before the final session of the talks in London on 5–6 December. Had de Valera been there on that last night, he could have stood up and led his team out of Downing Street if he wished. Instead, he left the decision to others.

In 1919 de Valera had been elected president of the ministry of the revolutionary assembly, Dáil Éireann. Sinn Féin had convened the Dáil that year for the first time, following the party's overwhelming victory in Ireland in the UK general election of 1918. Its MPs refused to sit in the UK parliament at Westminster. In August 1921 de Valera arranged for Dáil Éireann to reelect him as its president using the grander title 'President of the Irish Republic'. He had not yet become a divisive figure, being nominated as President of the Irish Republic by the Volunteer leader Commandant Seán Mac Eoin TD and seconded by Richard Mulcahy TD – both of whom spoke highly and even warmly of him, but would later support the agreement for a treaty made in London that de Valera was to reject.

In the Dáil that month, some ministers expressed unhappiness at de Valera's decision not to go to London. Minister for Local Government W.T. Cosgrave TD, later the first premier of the Irish Free State, said that de Valera 'had an extraordinary experience in negotiations. He also had the advantage of being in touch already.' This was, presumably, a reference to de Valera's talks about talks with Lloyd George shortly after the truce had been arranged. Cosgrave also said, 'The head of the State in England was Mr. Lloyd George and he expected he would be one of the plenipotentiaries on the side of England […] this was a team they were sending over and they were leaving their ablest player in reserve. Now it was not usual to leave the ablest players

31

in reserve. The reserve would have to be used some time or other and it struck him now was the time they were required.'

Minister for Finance Michael Collins TD also thought the president should be part of the delegation. Collins told the Dáil, 'He did not want to go himself and he would very much prefer not to be chosen.' De Valera replied that 'if he were not the symbol he would go' and that it was 'absolutely vital' Collins should be a member.

We can never know if Éamon de Valera would have achieved a better outcome had he been at the table in Downing Street from October to December 1921. When the Dáil later debated the proposed Treaty, one of the delegates in London displayed his impatience with what he saw as de Valera's second-guessing and hair-splitting over what might have been achieved. On 21 December 1921 Éamonn Duggan TD asked deputies, 'Does anyone here seriously suggest that the Dáil appointed five plenipotentiaries with their staffs and all the rest of it to go to London to ask the British Government to recognise the Irish Republic? Did it, or did it not?' De Valera responded cryptically to him with the words 'Act in association'. This was likely a reference to de Valera's earlier proposal for an 'external association' of Ireland with the Empire, instead of actual membership of that grouping of states under the Crown. British ministers saw this in effect as proposing a republic and repeatedly rejected it. Duggan retorted, 'We either went to London to ask for recognition of the Irish Republic or we went to compromise. There is no other alternative.' De Valera: 'There is.' Duggan replied, 'I know what is in the President's mind – external association. External association if it means anything means this, that you go to England and you say, "If you recognise the Republic, we will enter into some kind of alliance with you."' At which de Valera exclaimed, 'Hear, hear.'

Duggan was frustrated, 'That brings me back to what I said. You sent us to ask recognition of the Irish Republic or you did not – you did either one or the other. Now the President, when he gets up and makes one of his impassioned and eloquent speeches, creates a kind of smoke-screen of words, so that it is almost impossible to see out of it into the world of fact. Now, I am going to try to get to the facts. Who was responsible for the compromise? The whole Cabinet and the whole Dáil and the plenipotentiaries. We were all in the one boat. There is no use blinking the facts any longer.' Such exchanges would continue for years.

Why Dev Stayed at Home

In July 1921, immediately after a truce was agreed and the War of Independence was paused, de Valera went to London for talks with Lloyd George about possible negotiations. So why did he not return in October for those substantive talks themselves? He told the Dáil on 23 August 1921, 'The one chief reason I had in going myself to these preliminary negotiations [was that] I saw it gave me a definite opportunity to bring Ireland's case before the world.' He added that he would now stay at home, 'where I will be more valuable'. Others would be on the Irish team at the peace talks. He thought that 'it will be quite evident to the public the reason I do not want to be one of them is that the duties at home require my attention.' But his rationale for not facing the British prime minister at the negotiating table was anything but 'quite evident' to many people, then or later.

It is significant that – also in August, in the Dáil – de Valera admitted he foresaw 'proposals brought back which cannot satisfy everybody, and will not'. He said, 'my position is that when such a time comes I will be in a position, having discussed the matter with the Cabinet, to come forward with such proposals as we think wise and right. It will be then for you either to accept the recommendations of the Ministry or reject them. If you reject them you then elect a new Ministry. You would then be creating a definite active opposition.' He soon returned to the topic. With still no firm arrangement in place for substantive peace talks, de Valera said that 'he really believed it was vital at this stage that the symbol of the Republic should be kept untouched and that it should not be compromised in any sense by any arrangements which it might be necessary for our plenipotentiaries to make.' This was de Valera as the symbol of Ireland, unsullied by further intercourse in London. He further protested, somewhat defensively, 'It was not a shirking of duty.' (*Dáil debates*, 14 Sept. 1921).

De Valera knew well, from both the internal logic of events and from his meetings alone with Lloyd George in July, that there was no possibility of the British agreeing to Ireland simply leaving the Empire to become a republic, and still less a republic of all thirty-two counties on the island. Any agreement would have to involve compromise. The delegates were not going to gain fully what successful Sinn Féin parliamentary candidates had failed to win by their democratic victory in the 1918 and 1921 general elections, and what armed Volunteers had not won by physical force. Arthur Griffith reportedly told Fr Eugene Coyle of Belleek that de Valera had instructed him, before he left for London, to 'get the best price you can for the cow' (*Ulster Herald*, 13 Oct. 1923). In April 1922 Griffith informed the Dáil, 'When I was going to London Mr. de Valera said to me, "There may have to be scapegoats" [...] Collins and myself were willing to be scapegoats.'

An even darker scenario, which is purely speculative, is that de Valera thought that a breakdown in talks would be followed by the arrest of Sinn Féin leaders present in London. Ned Broy, escort and private secretary to Collins in 1921, was later to tell the Bureau of Military History (Witness Statement 1,280) that when officers at Volunteer Headquarters in Dublin learned that Collins was to be one of the Irish delegates, 'they were much perturbed at the possibility of Michael's being captured in London should the negotiations break down and thus a mortal blow would be delivered to the Irish Republican Army in its endeavour to carry on the renewed struggle.' A small aircraft was stood by at a London airfield to evacuate Griffith and the other delegates quickly in the event of negotiations collapsing at any point. Collins believed that the aircraft could just about reach Ireland with a five-passenger load. Broy said that 'On more than one occasion, when the negotiations were not going well, Collins laughingly asked me if I were prepared to fight my way out of London [...] I always felt that [...] it might be necessary to shoot our way out of the aerodrome.' Cabinet Secretary Thomas Jones noted an oddly ambiguous exchange between Collins and Lloyd George at their talks in London on 17 October when Collins complained that he had been shadowed when attending Mass the previous day. Lloyd George said, 'We have, of course, had to contemplate what to do in the event of a break, not as an act of menace but as an act of prudence.'

Or de Valera may simply have feared that any extended absence of himself, Griffith and Collins in London would make it easier for the most militant republicans to rally support and perhaps tempt some of them to break the Truce. Two of the seven Cabinet members (Brugha and Stack) were consistently hostile to the London talks, while three members (Griffith, Collins and

Barton) were among the five delegates away in London. This left only de Valera with W.T. Cosgrave at home to bridge the divide, if that is what the former wished to do.

During the negotiations, Irish delegates – on a number of occasions – asked de Valera to go to London. Replying to the Bureau of Military History in 1954 (Witness Statement 979), Barton recalled a visit to Dublin during the Peace Conference, 'I pressed de Valera to return with us to London on the score that it would be impossible for us to get the maximum terms without his being present and that it was unfair to expect us to get the best terms without his assistance. He was, however, unwilling to move from the decision which he had made earlier that he would stay here as being the last defence [...] I entirely agreed with the original decision, but thought it should have been reversed by the time we reached the final stage.' Had de Valera gone to London he could have told Lloyd George to 'go to the devil. I will not sign.' This, according to Erskine Childers, is what de Valera told the Cabinet meeting in Dublin on 8 December he would have done. Instead, absent on the night of 5–6 December 1921, he might merely criticise the decisions of others – decisions that caused them such anguish.

When Dáil Éireann debated the proposed Treaty, de Valera defended his absence from Downing Street, saying on 14 December that 'one of the reasons [...] was that the delegation should be provided against hasty action.' Then, later that month, writing to Joseph McGarrity in Philadelphia, he referred to the Irish delegates having asked him again to go over near the end, 'The British would think I had gone because I was anxious to prevent a breakdown. They would accordingly not make any further advance to me, but might stiffen instead [...] I probably would have gone over, nevertheless, had not Griffith [having] been shown that if he accepted the Crown he would split the country, given an express undertaking [de Valera's words underlined on the original] that he would not sign a document accepting allegiance but would bring it back and refer the matter to Dáil Éireann. This made us all satisfied; we were certain that Dáil Éireann would reject it' (De Valera Papers, UCD Archives, P150). In fact, the oath of allegiance required by the final agreement only pledged TDs to the future Constitution of the Irish Free State. Before the final session on 5 December, Griffith was to succeed in having allegiance replaced, in the case of the Crown, with an oath of faithfulness, so that TDs were to pledge, 'I solemnly swear true faith and allegiance to the Constitution of the Irish Free State as by law established and that I will be faithful to H.M. King George V., his heirs and successors.' This was a distinction that perhaps impressed few of his critics, but all five delegates, not only Griffith, signed up to the wording. It was part of the compromise.

In a centenary supplement published with the *Irish Times* on 25 May 2021, Bertie Ahern – a former leader of the Fianna Fáil party founded by de Valera in 1926, and a former prime minister (Taoiseach) between 1997 and 2008 – wrote that, 'given my strong Fianna Fáil background, people may be surprised to read that I think Dev was wrong not to lead the Irish delegation at the Treaty talks. The British team was highly skilled in negotiation [...] and it was not smart politics to leave the fledgling Dáil's leading statesman at home.' Ahern thought, 'This was a high risk and ultimately doomed strategy.' He added that he himself 'never for a second countenanced staying away from the negotiations' with Prime Minister Tony Blair that resulted in the Belfast 'Good Friday' Agreement.

Picking Plenipotentiaries

Plenus: Latin, meaning 'full'.
Potentia: Latin, meaning 'power'.
Plenipotentiarus: Latin, meaning 'plenipotentiary'.
Plenipotentiary: 'A borrowing from Latin. Invested with full authority, esp. so as to deputise for or represent a sovereign ruler; exercising absolute power.' (*OED*)

*

On the night of 5–6 December 1921, as the British piled pressure on the Irish at Downing Street, Prime Minister Lloyd George reminded the latter that they were there specifically as 'plenipotentiaries'. He said that 'it was now a matter of peace or war and we must each of us make up our minds.' So noted Robert Barton TD, who was acutely aware of the tension between the power inherent in the word 'plenipotentiary' and the demands of some of his Cabinet colleagues in Dublin.

It was de Valera himself who chose the term 'plenipotentiary' to describe the men who were sent to negotiate. Writing to Lloyd George on 23 August 1921, he expressed his revolutionary government's wish to end the conflict between Britain and Ireland, 'To negotiate such a peace, Dáil Éireann is ready to appoint its representatives, and, if your Government accepts the principle proposed, to invest them with plenary powers to meet and arrange with you for its application in detail.' On 14 September 1921, de Valera proposed to Dáil Éireann that five Sinn Féin members of the house 'be ratified as their plenipotentiaries' for possible peace talks with the British. He had studied Latin as a boy at Blackrock College, and even used Latin passages in correspondence when interned in Lincoln by the British. He did not need the *Oxford English Dictionary* to understand the word 'plenipotentiary'.

Having decided that he himself would not go to London, de Valera proposed five other members of the Dáil as plenipotentiaries. The Dáil ratified all five unanimously. De Valera, that day, also accepted that there could be 'arrangements which it might be necessary for our plenipotentiaries to make' that would compromise the symbol or aspiration of a full republic. Before the team left for London to begin peace talks, de Valera signed credentials for them on 7 October 1921:

> In virtue of the authority vested in me by Dáil Éireann I hereby appoint Arthur Griffith TD Minister for Foreign Affairs Chairman, Michael Collins TD Minister for Finance, Robert C. Barton TD Minister for Economic Affairs, Edmund J. Duggan TD, George Gavan Duffy TD as Envoys Plenipotentiary from the Elected Government of the Republic of Ireland to negotiate and conclude on behalf of

Ireland with the representatives of his Britannic Majesty, George V, a Treaty or Treaties of Settlement, Association and Accommodation between Ireland and the community of nations known as the British Commonwealth. IN WITNESS WHEREOF I hereunto subscribe my name as President.

Such credentials had a propaganda value but could never have been formally accepted by the British if presented to them formally. Their acceptance would have meant implicit British recognition of the delegates as representatives of all of Ireland and of the notional 'Republic of Ireland' itself. So the credentials were not formally presented at the Peace Conference. In an acrimonious exchange in the Dáil on 14 December 1921, de Valera used this fact to diminish the status of the representatives, who, from the outset, he himself had described as being 'plenipotentiaries' – which is to say, as being invested with full powers. Collins, responding defensively, told the Dáil that the credentials were in fact presented (but he did not say to whom, or if they were accepted). Griffith added, 'I believe Mr Lloyd George saw the document.' These public statements perturbed the British prime minister, who, according to his Cabinet secretary Thomas Jones, had not seen the credentials and thought, 'Had they been formally presented we should have had to reject them. They looked as if they had been drawn by de Valera to make difficulties.' The word 'formally' in that sentence may be significant. Perhaps Jones, or even Lloyd George, saw the credentials informally. Moreover, according to Barton's notes of the final session, Lloyd George himself then referred to the Irish delegates as 'plenipotentiaries' when it suited him. Another example of ambiguity related to the words 'negotiate and conclude [...] a Treaty' in the credentials. Deputies in the Dáil argued as to whether or not this meant that delegates might have dispensed altogether with Dáil approval, an entirely abstract point given that the agreement which the delegates actually concluded was explicitly an agreement *for* a treaty and that its terms made it subject to ratification separately by elected representatives on each side of the Irish Sea.

On the same day that de Valera issued their credentials, he also sent the five men separate instructions. Acknowledging that 'The Plenipotentiaries have full powers as defined in their credentials', he added that 'It is understood however that before decisions are finally reached on the main questions that a despatch notifying the intention of making these decisions will be sent to the Members of the Cabinet in Dublin and that a reply will be awaited by the Plenipotentiaries before the final decision is made.' He continued, 'It is also understood that the complete text of the draft treaty about to be signed will be similarly submitted to Dublin and reply awaited', and 'In case of a break the text of the final proposals from our side will be similarly submitted.' He concluded, 'It is understood that the Cabinet in Dublin will be kept regularly informed of the progress of the negotiations.' This memorandum had political rather than legal implications, for the Dáil had earlier ratified, without any qualifications, his nomination of the five men as plenipotentiaries. Indeed, de Valera did not now claim that the Cabinet had a power of veto, just that there was an 'understanding' that senior ministers in Dublin would be 'kept regularly informed'. In fact, in the course of the later debate on the proposed Treaty, on 14 December 1921, Arthur Griffith informed the Dáil that 'During the whole of the time we were there [in London] we sent every night a courier to Dublin, with details of everything that happened, to the President. I understand that copies were made.

I think there were five copies sent – one for each of the Ministers [at home], so that day by day each of them was acquainted with all that was going on, public conversations and private.' Many of those communications survive in the National Archives.

All substantial issues were also discussed at a long Cabinet meeting in Dublin two days before the final session of the Peace Conference. Back in London, at that final session, they exercised their powers as plenipotentiaries and signed an agreement – one that, under its own terms, still required the approval of members of the Dáil in Ireland before having the force of a treaty.

Five Go to London

F ive men went to England to negotiate an agreement to
end the War of Independence and establish an independent Irish state. Three of them were members of the Cabinet of the 2nd Dáil (1921–22). The Cabinet then consisted of
its president (de Valera) and six senior ministers (known officially in the British style as secretaries of state). There were also
eight junior ministers. These included Constance Gore-Booth
('Countess Markievicz' by marriage), who had been a member
of the Cabinet of the 1st Dáil but was reassigned by de Valera to
junior ministerial status in August 1921. 'Why didn't you send
me?' she was to ask the Dáil on 3 January 1922.

The collective experience of the plenipotentiaries was a broad
mosaic. Their chairman, **Arthur Griffith TD** (1871–1922),
founded the Sinn Féin movement in 1905. He was now the
Irish Minister for Foreign Affairs. He grew up in central Dublin,
his father bearing a long illness as the family struggled to make
ends meet. Born in 1871, Griffith was older than Collins and de

Valera. He was an ardent nationalist when young, active in cultural clubs and mentored by the veteran Fenian John O'Leary. A printer by trade, in 1899 he set up and edited – with Irish Republican Brotherhood backing – the weekly *United Irishman*. James Joyce was said, by his brother, to have described this as 'the only paper in Dublin worth reading.' It included a range of lively cultural, economic and political opinion. It boosted the early career of W.B. Yeats, who sometimes campaigned on particular issues with Griffith.

In 1904 Griffith wrote *The Resurrection of Hungary*, which became a best-selling pamphlet. Citing the constitution of the Austro-Hungarian Empire, Griffith signalled his willingness to retain a link with the British Crown in order to further the cause of an independent Irish parliament. But he was a republican, not a monarchist. Having launched his Sinn Féin movement, he struggled for years to keep both it and a series of advanced nationalist weekly papers going in the face of British suppression and Irish conservatism. He took part in the Howth gun running of 1914. He was not a pacifist, but he generally regarded violence as harmful to the poor and frequently counter-productive. He attended a small but key planning meeting organised by the IRB Supreme Council in September 1914, along with most of the future leaders of the 1916 Rising. He himself did not participate directly in that insurrection but, nonetheless, was interned after it.

In 1917 Griffith gracefully yielded the leadership of Sinn Féin to Éamon de Valera, who had escaped execution for his part in the 1916 Rising and whom militant Volunteers wished to see as the head of the party. Griffith remained active as de Valera's deputy, both in the party and in the new Dáil. In 1918 he was elected as a Sinn Féin MP for Cavan and for Tyrone. On 19

December 1921 Griffith told Dáil Éireann that, when acting as its substitute president in 1919–20 while de Valera was in the United States and the War of Independence raged at home, 'I had at least the responsibility on my shoulders of standing for all that was done in that defence, and I stood for it (applause). I would stand for it again under similar circumstances.'

Michael Collins TD (1890–1922), of the five plenipotentiaries, was the most senior political figure after Griffith. He was Minister for Finance. Up until January 1916 he had worked for a decade as a clerk in London. He became a leader of the armed struggle that, along with Sinn Féin's democratic victory in the 1918 general election, brought Britain to the negotiating table. As a Sinn Féin candidate, he was elected unopposed for the constituency of Cork County South in 1918. His heroic exploits and achievements are the stuff of legend, and many Irish people – including the present author's grandfather – boasted after Collins's death of having helped him in some way during the War of Independence. His good looks and personality added to his appeal. The 1996 Oscar-nominated biopic of Collins, directed by Neil Jordan – in which he was played by Liam Neeson and his girlfriend Kitty by Julia Roberts – enhanced his posthumous image.

Robert Childers Barton TD (1881–1975) was the third government minister in the group, holding a brief for economic affairs. His father was a Wicklow landowner; his mother, a daughter of Rev. Charles Childers (Her Majesty's chaplain at Nice and canon of Gibraltar). Robert's father is said to have fallen out irreconcilably with his neighbour and friend, the nationalist leader Charles Stewart Parnell, concerning the union between Britain and Ireland (*Dictionary of Irish Biography*).

Robert's staunchly Protestant and unionist family had an income not only from their 1,500 acres in Co. Wicklow but also from the French vineyards of Barton & Guestier, started by Thomas Barton in 1725. Educated at Rugby in England, Robert pursued studies as an agriculturalist before joining the Royal Dublin Fusiliers during the First World War – in which he lost two brothers. Following the executions of Irish rebels in 1916, he resigned his commission and was, in 1918, elected a Sinn Féin MP for Wicklow West. In December 1918 Barton, George Gavan Duffy and Seán T. O'Kelly – a future President of Ireland – went to London on behalf of Sinn Féin in an unsuccessful effort to meet the visiting US president, Woodrow Wilson.

Barton and his first cousin Erskine Childers, who was a secretary for the Irish at the Peace Conference in London, were both seen as hardline republicans. Nevertheless, Barton signed the agreement for a treaty on 6 December 1921 and criticised de Valera for not attending. He voted in the Dáil for the Treaty, but later joined de Valera and the anti-Treaty side.

George Gavan Duffy TD (1882–1951) was the son of an Irish nationalist politician who became premier of Victoria in Australia. His half-brother Frank was the chief justice of the Australian High Court. His mother died when he was 7, and he was reared by half-sisters at their family's villa in the south of France. He was educated at Stonyhurst College, a Jesuit boarding school in Lancashire.

In 1907 Gavan Duffy qualified as a solicitor in London, and in 1916 he acted for Roger Casement in his trial for high treason in England. F.E. Smith, who prosecuted Casement in that case, now sat as Lord Chancellor Birkenhead across the Peace Conference table from Gavan Duffy. After the Casement trial, Gavan Duffy moved to Ireland and was called to the bar. Elected a Sinn Féin MP for Dublin County South in 1918, he became the revolutionary Dáil's representative in Paris and later in Rome. In 1946 he was appointed president of the Irish High Court, in which capacity he enjoyed a good reputation professionally.

Éamonn Duggan TD (1874/9–1936) had been a law clerk in Co. Meath. He eventually became a solicitor, aged nearly 40. Although he participated in the 1916 Rising, he was not struck off the roll of solicitors; he resumed his practice after his release from internment in 1917. He was elected as a Sinn Féin MP for Meath South in 1918. Having been Director of Intelligence during the War of Independence, Duggan was interned again in 1920. Moved from Mountjoy Prison to a jail in Brixton, he was sometimes allowed out, as a member of parliament, to dine in the House of Commons. He was released in June 1921, and went to London as one of the back-up team when de Valera had talks about talks with Lloyd George there in July 1921.

On these men's shoulders, on the night of 5–6 December 1921, lay a great weight of responsibility to a nation worn down by war and hoping for both peace and the creation of an independent state. The number of people interned without charge in Ireland alone was estimated to be about three thousand (UK National Archives, CAB/23/17).

THE BRITISH TEAM

The Irish were up against a team led by one of the most remarkable British politicians of the twentieth century, Prime Minister David Lloyd George. His nickname was 'The Welsh Wizard', which was half compliment and half insult.

Griffith's widow later told Michael Hayes that her husband described to her Lloyd George entering a room, 'like a benevolent old gentleman with white hair and a smooth face showing no line on it'. She said that she had remarked, 'He must have an easy conscience.' Her husband replied, 'He has no conscience.'

Lloyd George needed to be politically astute. Although he was prime minister, the Liberals he led constituted the smaller partner in government with Conservative and Unionist Party MPs. Britain was struggling to recover from the First World War, and unemployment was high. When it came to Ireland, he faced fierce opposition to any radical concessions to republicans. A solid block of MPs, some known as 'Die-hards', was dedicated to backing unionism and the Empire robustly. No British government could realistically contemplate using its military to try to force Northern Ireland into a united Ireland under Sinn Féin. British officers in Ireland had already demonstrated a tendency to mutiny. Nor could a British government at that time survive if it agreed to any part of Ireland abandoning the Empire and Crown completely in order to become an entirely independent republic on Britain's doorstep.

Facing the five Irish delegates were seven British negotiators. Much of the work between October and December would be done not in full sessions but in smaller sub-conferences and meetings. This sometimes frustrated Gavan Duffy and Barton, but it was acceptable to de Valera, who had met Lloyd George alone for initial talks in July. The members of the powerful British team were as follows (senior UK ministers are known as secretaries of state):

Lloyd George (1863–1945), MP for Carnarvon Boroughs, prime minister 1916–1922. A Liberal. A Welsh Nonconformist by upbringing, and a solicitor by profession, he had an independent streak and opposed the Boer War (as Griffith had too). He introduced the Representation of the People Act that more than doubled the electorate for the general election of 1918, by giving women the vote and broadening the franchise for men. His effort to link the proposed introduction of military conscription in Ireland to the possible granting of Home Rule alienated the Irish and helped Sinn Féin to win support. His political career ended when his coalition government fell in October 1922, in part due to his agreeing to the Treaty.

F.E. Smith (1872–1930), MP for Liverpool West Derby, Lord Birkenhead, Lord Chancellor. A Conservative. A wealthy barrister, he was autocratic but professionally well regarded. Having campaigned against Irish Home Rule at the 1892 general election, he staunchly defended the right of Ulster unionists to opt out of government from Dublin. He supported Edward Carson at armed processions in Ulster that preceded the signing of the Ulster Covenant in 1912. He successfully prosecuted Roger Casement, who had conspired to import arms from Germany for Irish nationalists (in response to the importation of arms by Ulster unionists whom Smith supported) and who was then hanged for treason. However, Smith's role in agreeing the Treaty alienated Carson and others who had admired him.

Austen Chamberlain (1863–1937), MP for Birmingham West, Leader of the House of Commons, Conservative Party leader. Chamberlain studied history and became a politician early. His father was the Colonial Secretary Joseph Chamberlain, whose visit to Dublin in 1899 to promote the British Boer War was actively opposed in the streets by Arthur Griffith and his socialist friend James Connolly, along with Maud Gonne. Before the First World War, Chamberlain favoured a federal structure for the whole United Kingdom – or 'Home Rule All Round', as it was sometimes called. He was a strong defender of the British Empire. In 1920 he turned down an offer to be made Viceroy of India. Chamberlain alienated many in his own party by appearing to them to be too soft on the Irish during the Treaty negotiations. In October 1922 he was replaced as party leader by Bonar Law, a strong supporter of Ulster unionism.

Winston Churchill (1874–1965), MP for Dundee, Secretary of State for the Colonies. A Liberal, but previously a Conservative Unionist MP. Cavalry officer and war correspondent. Between the ages of 2 and 6, he had lived in the Phoenix Park, Dublin, where his grandfather was viceroy and where his nanny warned him against the Fenians. His father Randolph famously declared, 'Ulster will fight, and Ulster will be right.'

Laming Worthington-Evans (1868–1931), MP for Colchester, Secretary of State for War. A Conservative, but close to Lloyd George. A solicitor.

Hamar Greenwood (1870–1948), MP for Sunderland, Chief Secretary for Ireland. A Liberal. Born in Canada of Welsh descent, he worked in the Canadian Department of Agriculture before moving to Britain and becoming a barrister. During the Irish War of Independence, he publicly defended harsh reprisals by Crown forces.

Gordon Hewart (1870–1943), MP for Leicester East. Attorney-General. A Liberal. He had declined the positions of Secretary of State for Ireland and Home Secretary in favour of his legal career. In March 1922 he became Lord Chief Justice of England.

THE HOUSE IN HANS PLACE

A nice terraced house in Hans Place, London, went on sale recently for £16m, and a 'well-presented two-bedroom flat' for £2.4m. This is the fashionable West End. Hans Place is found variously described as being in Brompton, Knightsbridge, Kensington and Chelsea. From 8 October to 6 December 1921, number 22 Hans Place was home to the Irish delegates and their back-up staff. There is a photograph of Michael Collins standing on the house's back balcony, which overlooks Pont Street towards Cadogan Gardens – where number 15 was also rented for the Irish. Collins's energy is palpable.

The Dáil appears to have had few if any reservations about its delegates meeting the British at the heart of their empire. Just being seen to enter through the front door of 10 Downing Street gave them a certain status. They were like Daniel in the Lions' Den, in a city where all of the familiar comforts of home and the conveniences of one's office were at the disposal of the other side. 'As to procedure we are in your house and will follow your suggestions,' Griffith even told Lloyd George when invited by the prime minister at their first meeting to say how he wished to proceed.

Among the back-up team at Hans Place were four 'lady secretaries': Kathleen McKenna, Ellie and Alice Lyons, and Lily O'Brennan. According to McKenna, the wives of delegate Éamonn Duggan TD and Fionán Lynch TD 'acted as chaperones to the girls' on their trip to England. This did not preclude 'the girls' from attending an underground shooting range in London, where they learnt to use revolvers. It was probably an advisable precaution, for someone daubed the word 'MURDERERS' in big red letters on the public footpath at Hans Place.

Fionán Lynch himself was there to help with administration, as were Diarmuid O'Hegarty, Erskine Childers and John Chartres. All were described as 'secretaries' to the delegation. The head cook, Mrs Folkard, lived in London but hailed from McKenna's hometown of Oldcastle, Co. Meath. Housemaids, assistant cooks, cleaners and other household staff were employed by Art O'Brien, the Irish government's representative in London, who borrowed staff from the London Irish clubs and from the Self-Determination League.

Desmond FitzGerald, then the government's Minister for Publicity, travelled over too, and was available on the night of 5–6 December to give advice. His brother Frank worked in England and is said to have arranged the acquisition of weapons for the Irish at home during this period. Others visited Hans Place as advisors to the delegates. They included Timothy Smiddy, the Professor of Economics at University College Cork, who later became Ireland's envoy to the United States.

From Hans Place delegates sometimes went to the theatre, to restaurants such as the Frascati and to church. On many mornings Collins attended Mass, at Brompton Oratory or at St Mary's in Cadogan Street. He told his friend Kitty Kiernan that he lit candles for her there. Griffith liked long walks and sometimes strolled London's streets with members of his back-up team. Delegates were under great pressure.

There were rumours of heavy drinking and boisterous evenings at the Irish houses, although Kathleen McKenna later insisted that the delegation, 'at all times and under all circumstances, was highly circumspect in its comportment.' In 1954 Barton told the Bureau of Military History that 'I wouldn't say there was much justification for the charge that members of the staff of the Irish Delegation were having too good a time. We worked very hard [...] on the whole, I should say it was a very quiet and respectable and well-behaved delegation.' The Irish did pay for certain repairs, the nature of which suggested some horseplay within their rented houses.

The front of the house in Hans Place overlooks a communal garden of mature trees. Built into the park's railings, directly visible as one exits the front door of Number 22, is a fountain in polished pink granite. Erected in 1886, it is surmounted by a broken column. Such a column generally indicates life cut short – but formerly, too, was a Renaissance signifier of fortitude, which is one of the four cardinal virtues. The monument in Hans Place was erected in honour of an Englishman who lived nearby. Herbert Stewart (1843–1885) died trying to relieve the siege of Khartoum in the Sudan, when General Charles Gordon was killed there. Winston Churchill, Secretary of State and one of the men with whom Griffith, Collins and the others were negotiating in 1921, had himself served in the Sudan in the autumn of 1898 – when the British took bloody revenge for Gordon's death. For his part, Griffith composed a scathing ballad about Britain's behaviour in that war. His rousing 'Song of the Khalifa' appeared in the second issue of his *United Irishman* on 11 March 1899. He had written in the first issue, 'One cannot be an African "civiliser" and an Irish Nationalist.'

A broken column is also the most striking feature of the memorial above Arthur Griffith's modest grave in Glasnevin cemetery, a memorial erected by his widow. Did she get the idea for this when she recalled her visit to Griffith at 22 Hans Place, when she was photographed with him in the doorway there?

The Irish HQ during treaty talks in London: 22 Hans Place, as seen today from Cadogan Square. Collins was photographed standing on its balcony.

Visitors and Finance

As if he had not enough to do, Griffith was also asked to receive visitors at Hans Place. They included the playwright George Bernard Shaw, for whom Desmond FitzGerald's wife Mabel once worked as a secretary, and the controversial sculptor Jacob Epstein, who had designed the tomb for Oscar Wilde in Paris. Epstein arrived with a babe in arms.

Another visitor was James Joyce's friend Ezra Pound, a poet interested in economics. Pound later wrote, 'One of the most illuminating hours of my life was that spent in conversation with Griffith,' whom he called 'the inventor of Sinn Féin'. At one point, wrote Pound, Griffith exclaimed, 'All you say is true. But I can't move 'em with a cold thing like economics.' According to Pound's biographer David Moody, this remark would 'stay with Pound for the rest of his life, as a constant reminder that intelligence by itself did not bring about change.' Pound recalled the visit to Hans Place in *The Cantos*, where he describes Griffith as 'stubby' and refers to someone who appears to be a bodyguard:

And the stubby little man was up-stairs.
And there was the slick guy in the other corner reading
  The Tatler,
Not upside down, but never turning the pages,
And then I went up to the bed-room, and he said,
The stubby fellow: Perfectly true,
'But it's a question of feeling,
'Can't move 'em with a cold thing, like economics.'
And so we came downstairs and went out [...]

Griffith had a keen sense of Ireland's economic needs, and pressed to ensure that the Treaty secured real financial freedom for the new state. He had inundated readers of his papers with statistics. In the late twentieth century Prof. Paddy Lynch, a prominent civil servant and economist, acknowledged Griffith's grasp of economic and financial realities. Michael Laffan, too, points out in the *Dictionary of Irish Biography* that a distinguishing feature of Griffith's nationalism was 'his preoccupation with the economic aspects of Irish independence, his determination that Ireland should be a modern, prosperous state. He was a pragmatic man and was concerned with issues such as industrialisation, mining, afforestation, over-taxation, and the protection of Irish goods against foreign (specifically, British) competition.' Griffith had established the Sinn Féin Bank, having seen how Irish business and trade were long restricted by British rules, practices and prejudices.

The Treaty left Ireland financially freer in 1921 than could have been foreseen when Griffith launched Sinn Féin in 1905. It included provision for offsetting liability for a proportionate burden of the United Kingdom's debt by 'having regard to any just claim on the part of Ireland by way of set-off or counter-claim' arising historically. Besides any other considerations, this was intended to refer to the long-held concern that Ireland had been treated relatively unfairly when it came to matters of taxation and state expenditure within the United Kingdom. The Treaty's economic benefits, particularly in respect to fiscal autonomy, were obscured by acrimonious political arguments.

DE VALERA, FORCE AND ULSTER

Although de Valera did not go to London for the substantive peace talks, he expressed, no later than August 1921, some crucial thinking on issues that were to be addressed there. De Valera's views were neither as absolute nor as militant as his later violent opposition to the Treaty might lead people to believe.

On 10 August 1921, writing to Lloyd George, de Valera insisted, 'As regards the question at issue between the political minority [unionists] and the great majority of the Irish people, that must remain a question for the Irish people themselves to settle. We cannot admit the right of the British Government to mutilate our country, either in its own interest or at the call of any section of our population.' Nevertheless, he also then assured the British prime minister, 'We do not contemplate the use of force [...] We agree with you "that no common action can be secured by force".' De Valera could not resist adding, 'Our regret is that this wise and true principle which your Government prescribes to us for the settlement of our local problem it seems unwilling to apply consistently to the fundamental problem of the relations between our island and yours.' Griffith quoted these passages to Lloyd George at the fourth session of the Peace Conference in London, on 14 October 1921.

De Valera also told Dáil Éireann, 'if the Republic were recognised, he [de Valera] would be in favour of giving each county power to vote itself out of the Republic if it so wished. Otherwise they would be compelled to use force' (*Dáil debates*, 22 Aug. 1921). Many people came to believe that the Treaty split was centrally about partition. But, throughout 1921, there were clear indications that de Valera himself accepted that it was dangerous and futile to try to force unionists into a united Ireland. Instead, he wished to extract a high price for partition. The split in Sinn Féin, when it came, would be largely due to two factors: the Irish Free State's membership of the British Empire (Commonwealth) – with a continuing role for the King in respect to the Irish Free State – and the form of oath that deputies of the Irish Free State's Dáil would be obliged to take – one that pledged them to be faithful to the monarch.

In the Dáil debate of 22 August 1921, held privately behind closed doors, de Valera bluntly told deputies, 'They had not the power, and some of them had not the inclination, to use force with Ulster. He did not think that policy would be successful. They would be making the same mistake with that section as England had made with Ireland.' The Dáil debates' official report records him also telling his colleagues that day that 'He would not be responsible for such a policy. Ulster's present position was that she claimed the Six Counties as a constitutional right given to her constitutionally through the Realm and did not want to be under the domination of the rest of Ireland whose sentiments, ideals and religion were different.' His speech is relevant today, as unionists insist on their separate identity even while they may be about to become a minority in Northern Ireland. De Valera continued, 'Ulster would say she was as devotedly attached to the Empire as they were to their independence and that she would fight for one as much as they would do for the other. In case of coercion she would get sympathy and help from her friends all over the world.'

John Bowman notes in his *De Valera and the Ulster Question, 1917–73* (Oxford, 1982, p. 55) that de Valera's speech that day was 'met with dissatisfaction, apprehension, and confusion'. Deputies revealed 'a marked antipathy to the Ulster unionists'. But de Valera had glimpsed the future when he met Prime Minister Lloyd George four times in July 1921, and was aware of the military realities on the ground. Violent fantasies could not create a free state, never mind a thirty-two-county Irish republic.

Throne and Tyrone

Before the delegates left Dublin for London in October 1921, there was already a border between the six counties of Northern Ireland and the other twenty-six counties of the island. The Treaty did not create it, as is sometimes mistakenly thought. By July 1921, when the truce brought a pause in the hostilities of the War of Independence, Ireland was already partitioned. Northern Ireland had inaugurated its own working parliament under the British Government of Ireland Act 1920. The creation of a thirty-two-county republic was not on the table in London. Lloyd George had made this clear to de Valera in their talks of July 1921, and in correspondence that followed between July and October.

What the British were prepared to countenance was the creation of an independent all-Ireland dominion state that would be a member of the Commonwealth; it would be within the British Empire, and the King would be its symbolical head. During October and early November, the British negotiators in London even put some pressure on Northern Ireland to be part of such a new all-Ireland state. They envisaged Ireland as some kind of federation in which Northern Ireland would continue to have its own local status and a subsidiary parliament, similar to what it had enjoyed within the United Kingdom since May 1921. But unionists were determined that such an arrangement would not, under any circumstances, go ahead.

In August 1921, in Dáil Éireann, de Valera conceded that individual Irish counties in which unionists were in a majority could be allowed to opt out of a new Irish state. He still insisted on the 'essential unity' of Ireland, but this was a qualified type of unity that implicitly recognised practical limitations.

So if the right of unionists to secede from the rest of Ireland was conceded, would any of the six counties of the existing Northern Ireland in which nationalists were in a majority be likewise entitled to join the Irish Free State? A significant majority of voters in Fermanagh and Tyrone had chosen nationalist and republican candidates in the general election of May 1921 and might vote for their counties to become part of the Free State. Arthur Griffith and Michael Collins believed that this would happen. They also foresaw some other border districts in which there were nationalist majorities, including south Armagh and parts of Derry, leaving Northern Ireland as well. They believed that if and when this occurred, the remaining portion of Northern Ireland would not be viable – that its government would later decide to join the Irish state for economic reasons. A mechanism for achieving what they wanted, the Boundary Commission, was written into the Treaty.

Protestants, overwhelmingly unionist, constituted an overall majority of the population in the nine counties of the old Irish province of Ulster, but it was not a comfortable majority. For that reason, the UK parliament created Northern Ireland out of six of those counties so that a majority of two Protestants to every one Catholic might ensure constitutional predictability. On 17 October 1921 Arthur Griffith shared with the British negotiators in London the following population statistics. Whole of Ulster (nine counties): 890,000 Protestants, 700,000 Catholics. Northern Ireland (six counties): 820,570 Protestants, 429,161 Catholics.

The British believed that when it came to public opinion at home and abroad, they were on weak ground in respect to the existing Irish border. For that reason, they did not want the Peace Conference to break down on the issue. If there was to be a break, they wished that it would come from the Irish appearing to be extremist and unreasonable in respect to the symbol of the Crown and the status of the Empire, both of which meant so much to Britain and to some existing dominions, such as Australia and Canada.

Lloyd George privately expressed surprise that de Valera had not pressed him on Fermanagh and Tyrone at their meetings in July 1921. In a contemporary diary, not published until 1971, Cabinet Secretary Thomas Jones described a revealing discussion that took place at a Cabinet meeting on 7 September 1921. Lloyd George – to the disgruntlement of some of his ministers – had summoned them to Inverness in northern Scotland when he was on vacation near there. Referring to de Valera, the prime minister told them, 'I was greatly relieved to go through the conversations with him without Tyrone and Fermanagh being raised. He was an unskillful negotiator but you cannot always count on his being maladroit.'

According to Jones, Lloyd George also told his Cabinet that if Britain were to give in and yield too much, 'It will give the impression that we have lost our grip, that the Empire has no further force and will have an effect in India and throughout Europe.' He thought that 'without acceptance of Throne and Empire you march into the bog.' He predicted how a conversation might go at future peace talks (taking it for granted then that de Valera would attend them):

> He says – 'What about Tyrone and Fermanagh?'
>
> Shall I say – 'Tyrone and Fermanagh are already in the Northern area?'
>
> De Valera says – 'What about your representative principle?'
>
> De Valera will talk about Tyrone and Fermanagh and the break will come on forcing these two counties against their will. Men will die for the Throne and Empire. I do not know who will die for Tyrone and Fermanagh. The feeling for Ulster is not as strong as in 1913/14. Lots feel a bit annoyed about Ulster, think them unreasonable, narrow. You will divide the nation [...] you may get a majority against you.

A century later, Tyrone and Fermanagh are still part of Northern Ireland. The hopes of Collins and Griffith were to be dashed in that respect. After their deaths in 1922, the Boundary Commission did not deliver what the two men had expected.

'Personal' Assurances

The Treaty negotiations dragged on for nearly two full months. Much of the final framework was clear to both governments no later than the start of November. At Lloyd George's request, and in consultation with the British, Griffith then delivered certain 'assurances'. These referred to the British Crown, Northern Ireland and naval defence, and indicated what remained to be agreed.

Although described as 'personal', the assurances were in fact conveyed in an official letter of 2 November that Griffith sent after he had discussed them with the other plenipotentiaries. Gavan Duffy and Barton were both unhappy about his sending such a letter, and numerous alterations were made to it before it went. Nonetheless, sent it was – as an official communication. De Valera did not object to it. Significant in their own right, the assurances are also important because on the night of 5–6 December, Lloyd George referred to Griffith's assurances in a manner that caused confusion both then and later. Whether or not he did so deliberately in order to muddy the waters is uncertain, but it may be noted that the British had ostensibly leaked a truncated version of Griffith's letter of 2 November to give the impression that he had yielded to British demands then (Owen McGee, *Arthur Griffith* [Dublin, 2015], pp. 265–6). On 3 November the London *Times* had cited 'usually well-informed sources' for its misleading suggestion that 'Sinn Féin is prepared to abandon its claim to independence.'

There were in fact significant qualifications to the assurances of 2 November. First, Griffith made a specifically *personal* promise to recommend proposals in certain circumstances. This bound none of the other delegates to agree with him. Secondly, the so-called 'formula' defining what would constitute 'a free partnership of Ireland with the other States associated within the British Commonwealth' was ambiguous. Thirdly, references to the 'essential unity' of Ireland and to the 'North East of Ireland' still left 'for further discussion' the determination of the precise boundaries and status of Northern Ireland. De Valera – in August 1921, in the Dáil – had conceded that counties with unionist majorities might opt out of an independent state. Fourthly, Griffith gave his assurances on the basis that he would be 'satisfied on other points' that were not fully identified in the letter itself.

Griffith's letter opened with him recalling that 'In our personal conversation on Sunday night you stated that three things were vital – our attitude to the British Commonwealth, the Crown and Naval Defence. You asked me whether, provided I was satisfied on other points, I would give you personal assurances in relation to these matters.' On naval defence, in respect to which Britain ultimately had the use of three Irish ports until 1938, there was no great stumbling block. Griffith noted that 'The objects of the British Government in regard to the Navy and the Air Force are and will remain purely defensive. None of their stipulations is intended in the smallest degree to afford either armed occupation or political control of any part of Ireland.' He continued, 'I agreed consequently to recommend that the British Navy should be afforded such coastal facilities as may be necessary pending an agreement similar to those made with the Dominions providing for the assumption by Ireland of her own coastal defence.'

Less straightforward was the relationship, if any, of Ireland to the Crown. The British were insisting that Ireland remain within the British Empire as a member of the Commonwealth – and therefore, at least nominally, under the King as the ultimate head of state. An oath must also be taken to the King. A long and unhappy relationship between England and Ireland framed the British monarchy in a highly problematic way, given its association with religious, political and military oppression. So an oath of any kind pledging allegiance or faithfulness to the King would likely stick in the throat of Sinn Féin members of Dáil Éireann. On 21 December, in the Dáil, Gavan Duffy was to describe the King as 'a gentleman who necessarily symbolises in himself the just anger and the just resentment of this people for 750 years [...] If they had kept their King out of Ireland an honest settlement would have been easy.' Ned Broy later told the Bureau of Military History, 'The mere expression "British Empire" compressed into itself the concentrated hatred of Irish nationalists.'

In his letter of 2 November, Griffith assured Lloyd George that – provided he was 'so satisfied' on 'other points' that included financial relations and recognition of 'the essential unity of Ireland' – he was prepared to recommend 'a free partnership of

Ireland with the other States associated within the British Commonwealth, the formula defining the partnership to be arrived at in later discussion'. He was, 'on the same condition, prepared to recommend that Ireland should consent to a recognition of the Crown as head of the proposed association of free States'. This qualification even left room for de Valera's view that Ireland might be a republic externally associated with the Commonwealth in a special new arrangement that merely recognised the Crown as head of that Commonwealth with which Ireland would have a third-party relationship. British negotiators always insisted on Ireland's membership of the Commonwealth itself.

Griffith stated clearly that 'this attitude of mine was conditional on the recognition of the essential unity of Ireland.' The term 'essential unity' also remained undefined. He added, 'As to the North East of Ireland, while reserving for further discussion the question of area, I would agree to any necessary safeguards and to the maintenance of existing parliamentary powers, and would agree that its industrial life should not be hampered or discriminated against in any way.'

Griffith told de Valera by letter next day, 'The tactical course I have followed has been to throw the question of Ulster against the questions of Association [with the Empire] and the Crown.' Griffith added that British ministers had assured him that if 'Ulster' proved unreasonable, they were 'prepared to resign rather than use force against us'. The Northern Ireland government in fact proved most obstinate, but British ministers never resigned.

On 9 November, writing from Dublin, de Valera complimented Griffith on how 'admirably' the delegation had managed to ensure that any possible breakdown would focus on Ulster's position rather than on Sinn Féin's objections to the new state being bound to the Empire and Crown. Nonetheless, he cautioned that 'The danger now is that we should be tempted, in order to put them more hopelessly in the wrong, to make further advances on our side. I think, as far as the "Crown and Empire connection" is concerned, we should not budge a single inch from the point where the negotiations have now led us.' He neither specified the point to which he thought negotiations had in fact led nor indicated when, if ever, the delegation might make any further compromise necessary to reach an agreement.

The assurances in Griffith's letter of 2 November should be distinguished from Griffith's further use of the term 'personal assurances' in letters of 23 November and 4 December to de Valera. On these dates he used it to refer back to a promise he made on 12 November to Lloyd George: not to oppose publicly for some days the British government's efforts to get the Northern Ireland government to indicate whether it either agreed to an all-Ireland state of some kind or else was prepared to face changes to the Irish border by means of a boundary commission. The nature of Griffith's promise on 12 November, and Thomas Pakenham's particular interpretation of it in his influential book *Peace by Ordeal*, will be considered later in the context of Lloyd George's explosive use of Griffith's assurances on the night of 5–6 December 1921.

Redrawing the Border

Had it worked as Collins and Griffith hoped, the Boundary Commission would have changed the map of Ireland. With the island already partitioned by Britain in 1920, Collins and Griffith, in 1921, wanted large nationalist communities in Northern Ireland to be permitted to opt out and join the Irish Free State. Until the very last night, in an effort to extract the best deal, Griffith carefully reserved the position of the Irish delegates on the proposal.

The idea of appointing a boundary commission was first raised before 1920, during discussions then about the possible partition of the island. Lloyd George referred to this fact when Michael Collins complained on 17 October 1921 that the border of Northern Ireland – as defined by the UK Government of Ireland Act 1920 – was unfair. According to Lloyd George's Cabinet secretary Thomas Jones, the prime minister replied that it was actually Irish representatives at Westminster who first insisted that the border not embrace the entire province of Ulster but embrace just six of its nine counties, 'The logical unit would have been Ulster. Your predecessors [who were not Sinn Féin MPs] said that was unfair because of the homogenous Catholic population in North-West Ulster [*i.e.* Co. Donegal].' The prime minister added, in an observation emblematic of the entire process in which the negotiators were also involved in 1921, 'We made a compromise; no compromise is logically defensible' (Jones, *Whitehall Diary*, iii, 135).

A boundary commission provision for inclusion in the Treaty was drafted in early November 1921. On 8 November the British official Lionel Curtis delivered a private memorandum to his side suggesting a way forward. It included such a commission. The idea was inspired, to an extent, by a provision in the Treaty of Versailles 1919 that was being used during 1921 to delimit the Silesian border between Germany and Poland. Also on 8 November, Cabinet Secretary Thomas Jones mentioned the idea of the Boundary Commission to Griffith and Collins, but did not yet say that the prime minister favoured it. Griffith, that same day, reported to de Valera that the British were proposing 'a boundary commission to delimit "Ulster", confining this Ulster to its existing powers. This would give us most of Tyrone, Fermanagh, and part of Armagh, Down, etc.' Griffith added, 'We did not give any definite opinion on the matter. It is their look-out for the moment. Jones is to see us again tomorrow.'

On the next day Griffith returned with another delegate, Éamonn Duggan TD. Griffith then told Jones, 'It is not our proposal, but if the Prime Minister cares to make it we would not make his position impossible. We cannot give him a pledge but we will not turn him down on it. We are not going to queer his pitch. We would prefer a plebiscite [where people could simply vote by district or county to join the Free State], but in essentials a Boundary Commission is very much the same. It would have to be not for Tyrone and Fermanagh only but for the six counties.'

Jones noted in his diary that later on 9 November, Lloyd George told him that the Boundary Commission would be for the *nine* counties of Ulster. This meant that it could also permit some unionist districts of the proposed Irish Free State to opt into Northern Ireland. Jones added, 'I told him that I certainly had not made that clear. That I had spoken of six counties.' It was an important distinction. Collins and Griffith appear to have assumed throughout that a delimiting boundary commission would in practice limit Northern Ireland to a smaller portion of the six counties, consistent with the wishes of people living there – but they did not seem to anticipate the possibility that unionist districts in Cavan, Monaghan and Donegal might opt *into* Northern Ireland, as Lloyd George did. Yet adjustments to the border envisaged in a British draft memo for presentation to the Northern Ireland parliament on 10 November did also reference nine counties (UK National Archives CAB 43/2/4/102).

In his private diary, Jones wrote that near midnight on 10 November, when a meeting of the committee to monitor the Irish truce had ended, he told Éamonn Duggan (who was on that committee) to tell Griffith that in the prime minister's mind 'a Boundary Commission should apply not to the 6 Counties only but to the 9 Counties of Ulster.' It is not known if Duggan did so.

On the evening of 9 November 1921, Griffith had again written to de Valera, briefing him, 'Lloyd George proposes [...] that a Boundary Commission to delimit the six-county area be established so as to give us the districts in which we are a majority.' Jones 'asked us did we think the "Ulstermen" would accept this proposal. We said we were quite sure they would not. He said that was his own opinion. The move was a tactical one to deprive "Ulster" of support in England by showing it was utterly unreasonable in insisting to coerce areas that wished to get out. He asked us would we stand behind such a proposal. We said that it would be their proposal – not ours, and we would not, therefore, be bound by it but we realised the value as a tactical manoeuvre and if Lloyd George made it we would not queer his position. He was satisfied with this.' Griffith hoped that the proposal would induce Northern Ireland to negotiate a united Ireland. He thought that if it did not, then at least Northern Ireland would be reduced in size and might before long prove to be unviable outside a united Ireland.

Then, on 12 November, Lloyd George himself met Griffith over lunch, at the house of his parliamentary private secretary Philip Sassoon MP. They discussed the letter that Lloyd George intended sending to Northern Ireland's prime minister, James Craig, in reply to the unionists' recent refusal to join an all-Ireland state under any circumstances. The letter as drafted included the full text of the page that Lloyd George was to flourish on 5 December, when he reportedly claimed both that 'Arthur Griffith had agreed to its contents' on 12 November and that Griffith had 'undertaken not to let him down'. The text that he flourished, including its proposal for a boundary commission, will be discussed later when Lloyd George's dramatic use of it is considered below.

After his lunch with the prime minister, Griffith once more briefed de Valera, 'Lloyd George and his colleagues are sending a further reply to the Ulstermen [...] offering to create an All-Ireland Parliament, Ulster to have the right to vote itself out within 12 months, but if it does a Boundary Commission to be set up to delimit the area.' Griffith informed de Valera that he had again reacted carefully to this, 'I told him it was his proposal, not ours. He agreed, but he said that when they were fighting next Thursday with the Die-hards [MPs strongly against concessions to Irish republicans] and "Ulster" in front, they were lost if we cut the ground away behind them by repudiating the proposal. I said we would not do that, if he meant that he thought we would come out in public decrying it. It was his own proposal. If the Ulstermen accepted it, we would have to discuss it with him in the privacy of the Conference.' Griffith assured de Valera that he also told Lloyd George that day, 'I could not guarantee its acceptance, as, of course, my colleagues knew nothing of it yet. But I would guarantee that while he was fighting the "Ulster" crowd we would not help them by repudiating him. This satisfied him. They are to send this letter on Monday.' Griffith had encouraged Lloyd George to proceed with the proposal, but had merely assented to giving him time to send the letter and to get a reply before the Irish responded.

Eleven days later, on 23 November, Griffith reported to de Valera that at a further meeting earlier that day, Lloyd George declared that 'On Ulster […] I had assured him I would not let him down […] I said I had given him that assurance and I now repeated it, but I told him at the time it was his proposal – not ours […] He was satisfied. He had misunderstood us in this instance and said as much.' The reference on 23 November to an earlier 'assurance' appears to be to their discussion of 12 November. As already seen, Griffith's verbal assurance on that day, like his earlier written 'personal assurances' of 2 November, had been carefully qualified.

On 4 December Griffith was to reiterate his position yet again, informing de Valera in a letter that, at yet another meeting in

London, this one attended also by Barton and Gavan Duffy, he had told Lloyd George that the Irish did not take any responsibility for the current British proposals on Ulster, 'They were theirs, not ours. They agreed but said that if Ulster refused them they intended, nevertheless, to go on with them. I had said I would not let them down on them [their Ulster proposals] as against Craig. I confirmed this. I had given them my personal assurances but we were not responsible for putting them forward and could not be placed in such a position. They agreed.'

It is not clear why Jones had initially thought that a boundary commission might only subtract from the territory of Northern Ireland. He later noted in his diary that at a British Cabinet meeting on 6 December 1921, about twelve hours after the agreement for a treaty was signed, 'it had been represented [he did not say by whom] that a Boundary Commission would possibly give Ulster more than she would lose.' Allowing for the fact that Lloyd George was then engaged in selling the Treaty to members of his own Cabinet who had not been involved in negotiations and also to a somewhat hostile parliament, this representation – even if exaggerated – indicated a British determination to ensure that the Boundary Commission would at least cut both ways.

Indeed, the wording of Article 12 of the proposed Treaty referring to the Boundary Commission – as laid before the whole Cabinet in Dublin in the week before the agreement was signed in London – implicitly permitted inclusion as well as exclusion. For it authorised the Boundary Commission 'to determine [...] the boundaries between Northern Ireland and the rest of Ireland'. Any ambiguity in Article 12 should have been obvious to all delegates and members of the Cabinet, and to their lawyers and advisors. Nobody appears to have proposed restricting the scope of the Boundary Commission by confining its brief to the exclusion of areas from Northern Ireland.

In 1954 Barton told the Bureau of Military History, 'I rather imagine that Lloyd George did not intend to let Griffith and Collins down so badly, but who knows? As a negotiator he was unreliable. If the boundary clause had been clarified in the final document and if it had been stated in the boundary clause that voting for exclusion or inclusion in the Free State must be by specific areas, as agreed verbally, then it would have been impossible to throw overboard the proposed plebiscite and exclusion or inclusion of large territories. Here is where Griffith and Collins made their biggest mistake [...] I think Collins was at that time almost prepared to go to war; he was no partitionist – nor for that matter was Griffith.'

In the event, Northern Ireland was not a party to the Treaty, and did not assent to the Boundary Commission despite Griffith's efforts to have Craig's response delivered before an agreement was signed. This was to prove problematic. The Irish Civil War also fatally delayed the commission. The hopes of Griffith and Collins that at least the counties of Fermanagh and Tyrone would join the Irish Free State were to be dashed. The possibility that the commission might allow unionist communities in the Irish Free State to join Northern Ireland alarmed the new government in Dublin. The Irish border has stayed as it was when first established in 1920, before the Treaty talks began.

Conjugal Visits

We may never know for certain if the Chicago-born Hazel Lavery, whose husband John painted portraits of the Irish delegates in London, had an affair with Michael Collins, as some claim she did. If so, then he exposed himself to blackmail. The fact that the married Lloyd George had a mistress for many years seems to excite people less than do rumours about the unmarried Collins.

Leaving gossip aside, there was a simpler way in which the emotional and physical aspects of relationships had a bearing on the peace talks. Already under great pressure to achieve an acceptable outcome, the Irish delegates worked in London for two months without their families. Wives and partners could join them at their rented accommodation, but this was not necessarily an easy or practical option. Short trips back to Ireland were likewise tiring and inconvenient. When Lloyd George, in September 1921, had summoned his ministers to a special Cabinet meeting about Ireland in Inverness, near where he was on holidays in the Scottish Highlands, Austen Chamberlain declared himself 'furious'. Yet here were the Irish on English home turf, expected to share rented houses with many others while their families were at home across the Irish Sea. For this and other reasons, it might have been better had the Irish simply returned to Dublin between carefully spaced rounds of negotiation.

Some wives came to London at the outset – Éamonn Duggan's, for example. Collins sorely missed his friend Kitty Kiernan, as their published correspondence demonstrates. When she visited 'Ans Plice' – her jocose, mock-Cockney spelling of the London address in a letter to Collins – there was great excitement. Kathleen McKenna later described a shopping expedition by herself, Kitty and Kitty's sister to select a dress that would please 'his fiancé', 'We three girls spent a very happy afternoon in Selfridges and Bourne and Hollingsworth's where we made many purchases.' Kathleen thought that 'Mick was very much in love with Kitty, and if God had spared Mick they would have been a happy married couple.'

Griffith and his wife had married late, partly for financial reasons. Although writers often refer to her as Maud, he addressed her as Mollie, or Molly. She called him Dan, a nickname used in his childhood by his family. Four warm love poems that Griffith wrote to Mollie under that name, when they were younger, survive in the National Library of Ireland. It may not be entirely coincidental that James Joyce, who was grateful for advice received from Griffith but also sceptical of aspects of the nationalist movement, gave the main female character in *Ulysses* the same first name as that of the Irish statesman's wife.

Griffith was eager for Mollie to come to London, 'at least for a few days', and eventually persuaded her to do so. If she was nervous about travelling on her own, she might accompany his friend Oliver St John Gogarty, otherwise known as 'Buck Mulligan' in Joyce's *Ulysses*. Gogarty was due to cross to London the following Saturday. Griffith wrote to her, 'Dear Mollie, I want you here; if you can even only come for a few days. As to outfit, etc., come here and I'll provide it; as to money, if you haven't enough get it from Mr Murphy and I'll get you any money you need when you are here. Surely you can send the children to Kelly's or some other family for a week. As to expense, I'll provide that. Do come.' Five days later, from a foggy London on 22 November, he was still pleading, 'If we are here to the end of the week, come over please [...] and stay at least for a few days.' In the same letter, he sympathised with their daughter Ita on the death of her pet rabbit, and expressed the hope that his son Nevin was practising a collection of conjuring tricks that Griffith had sent him from London, 'If I can get time one day I'll see if there are any more in London' (National Library of Ireland, MSS 49,530/8/2–3).

Mollie came in the end, although she did not share his great interest in politics. 'First thing I noticed in London was his hair turning white,' she wrote a few days later, 'I feel so worried.' Griffith had been ill when imprisoned earlier that year; during their weeks in London, Collins expressed concern about his chairman's health. Padraic Colum, to whom Griffith's widow spoke for his biography of her husband decades later, quoted her saying that Griffith promised her on the night that the Treaty was signed in London, 'You will have your wish [...] In August I will be out of politics.' It was an accurate forecast, although his departure was not to be as he had anticipated it.

DASH TO DUBLIN, 2–3 DECEMBER

J ust two days before the final, heated session of the peace
talks, the five plenipotentiaries attended a difficult meeting
of the Cabinet in Dublin. Erskine Childers TD (a secretary
to the delegates) and Kevin O'Higgins TD (Assistant Minister for Local Government) were permitted to attend at intervals
and to address the Cabinet.

Pressure had been mounting on the Irish in London. Griffith
and Collins had been invited to go to the prime minister's country residence at Chequers on the night of Monday, 28 November. As Collins had not yet returned from a quick trip to Dublin,
Duggan went instead. The two men were ushered into the Long
Room to meet Birkenhead and Sir Robert Horne, Chancellor
of the Exchequer, and Lloyd George. The prime minister had
earlier remarked to his Cabinet secretary on 'the appropriateness
of the chamber', which was 'very much as it was in the days of
Cromwell'; it was adorned with Oliver Cromwell's great sword
and a letter from Cromwell proclaiming, after the battle of Mar-

ston Moor, that 'The Lord made them as stubble in our hands.' Next day Griffith wrote to de Valera that the British intended to send their final proposals to Sir James Craig, the Northern Ireland premier, 'They agreed to send us them [informally] on Thursday evening [1 December], but formally to hand them to us on Tuesday [6 December]. It is essential a Cabinet meeting should be held. I shall return to Dublin on Friday morning and hope to see you on that evening. Please have a Cabinet meeting arranged for Saturday morning [3 December], when we shall be all there. I intend to return to London on that evening.'

Craig was not enhancing the mood. He spoke in the parliament of Northern Ireland that same week, publicly saying that he and Lloyd George had agreed as follows before he left London, 'By Tuesday next either the negotiations will have broken down or the Prime Minister will send me new proposals for consideration by the Cabinet.' Craig added, 'one more week only is given to say "Yes" or "No". That means that Sinn Féin, fully alive as it is now to our unflinching determination not to go into an All-Ireland Parliament, has got to say she will still work for a settlement or the negotiations are broken down.'

In time for the planned Cabinet meeting in Dublin's Mansion House, the Irish received from Lloyd George, as expected, the current draft of the Treaty, which he was prepared to show Craig and submit to parliament. Worn down by weeks of negotiation and political pressure from all sides, delegates endured on the evening of Thursday, 1 December 1921 what the *Irish Independent* described as a 'most exacting' session with the British about the latter's new proposal. The session dragged on very late as documents were redrafted. The *Irish Times* reported that 'Between 6.30 and midnight the tension was at its highest, and it constitutes the most strenuous period of any during the negotiations.' The two sides carefully considered and amended the proposal, clause by clause. 'The examination of the proposals was a sharp battle of wits between Mr Griffith and Mr Lloyd George,' remarked a correspondent in the *Freeman's Journal.* It was well past midnight by the time that the British and Irish finalised a draft document for further discussion.

To get to the meeting in Dublin – scheduled for eleven in the morning on Saturday, 3 December – and back to London early next day, as was required, the Irish had to make a tiring return journey by rail and mailboat that usually involved twenty-two hours' solid travel – eleven in each direction. For Collins, Griffith and Barton, it was the second such journey in eight days. Having been engaged by the British into the early hours of the morning of Friday, 2 December, Irish negotiators later that day left for Ireland. It was perhaps a sign of their tiredness or distraction that Griffith at one point left his draft of the British proposals in an unlocked briefcase in the dining-car of his train to Holyhead. Fortunately for him, an official rescued it before it fell into other hands.

Michael Collins, George Gavan Duffy and Erskine Childers had to leave London after Griffith, with Collins needing to collect a certain report from the prime minister's office. While he waited for it, he picked up a sheet of notepaper headed '10 Downing Street' and began one of his frequent letters to Kitty Kiernan. Collins and the others intended to catch an overnight mailboat that would leave them just a few hours to spare before the Cabinet meeting in Dublin on Saturday morning, but these were important hours because he intended to use them to brief senior figures in the armed struggle. His vessel, the *Cambria*, was on its maiden voyage, and the captain may have been eager to impress. It left Holyhead at 3.12 a.m., and was soon at full speed just off the coast of Wales when, at 3.28 a.m., it rammed and cut in two the *James Tyrel* from Arklow ('as if it were a piece of cheese', according to one report). Three of the schooner's crew died. In yet another of those half-heroic, half-humorous stories that accrued to Michael Collins, it is said that he helped to lower the *Cambria*'s lifeboats and offered the delegates' rooms on board to those rescued. He is also said to have refused a life-belt, remarking with a smile, 'I have been in tighter corners than this, and got out of them.' Among other passengers on board that night was a 27-year-old John Ford, later director of the quintessential Irish-American film *The Quiet Man* (1952). He was the son of an Irish emigrant whose home district Ford was to find badly damaged by Crown forces.

After the collision, the captain of the *Cambria* brought his vessel back to Holyhead. Its passengers were subsequently trans-ferred to the *Hibernia*, which left for Ireland at 7.50 a.m. and arrived at 10.31 a.m. This meant that Collins and the others had to dash straight to the Cabinet meeting. It lasted all day long, before they returned to London. There was no chance for Col-lins to have his planned prior meeting with the military men. Horace Plunkett called on Erskine Childers that day and found that 'He, who arrived this morning and goes back [to London] tonight, looked very tired.' If Childers, as their secretary, was exhausted, what of the delegates themselves? In 1935, in his well-known account of the Treaty negotiations, *Peace by Ordeal*, Frank Pakenham described them as 'a desperately tired and hag-gard little party when they arrived at the Mansion House' for the meeting.

Confused and Inconclusive

The Cabinet meeting lasted from eleven in the morning until seven in the evening on Saturday, 3 December. It exposed strains. De Valera had been out on the Atlantic seaboard giving pep talks to armed Volunteers in case the War of Independence resumed; he seemed irritated to have to interrupt his schedule to come back to Dublin and complained of being 'very tired'. Griffith had written to him on 29 November, after meeting Lloyd George in Chequers, 'It is essential a Cabinet meeting should be held. I shall return to Dublin on Friday morning and hope to see you on that evening. Please have a Cabinet meeting arranged for Saturday morning, when we shall be all there. I intend to return to London on that evening.' De Valera told Joe McGarrity, 'I was suddenly summoned to meet Griffith and the plenipotentiaries who had returned' (De Valera Papers, UCD Archives).

There were ambiguities and disagreements in respect to the proceedings of that vital Cabinet meeting that would allow the outcome to be interpreted in various ways. The short contemporary notes of it, made by acting Cabinet secretary Colm Ó Murchadha, are unsatisfactory (National Archives, Dáil Éireann 2/304/1).

On the table was the latest British proposal, received in writing by the Irish in London just two and a half days earlier. In August de Valera had told the Dáil that Ulster counties might opt out of an independent Ireland, but he now told his Cabinet colleagues that he could not sign 'any document which would give N[orth] E[ast] Ulster power to vote itself out of the Irish State'. Yet he added – as noted by Ó Murchadha – that, 'with modifications', the proposed agreement 'might be accepted honourably, and he would like to see the plenipotentiaries go back and secure peace if possible.' This may be an example of what John Bowman, in his book on de Valera and the Ulster question, described as de Valera's 'genius for the bespoke formula'. For the president seems to have left it to the plenipotentiaries to work out what those adequate 'modifications' might be. If he would not give Northern Ireland as a whole the right to remain in the United Kingdom, would he still be willing to let individual northern counties do so? Certainly, he 'would like to see' the delegates secure peace 'if possible', he said, but the final line of the official note records that he still did not wish to lead them, 'It was decided that the President would not join the Delegation in London at this stage of the Negotiations.' The passive form 'it was decided' leaves it unclear how that decision was made, and by whom.

The official notes list 'views' expressed at the meeting but record only three clear decisions reached at it, one of which was that de Valera would not go to London. The two further decisions were that delegates were empowered to meet Craig if they wished (which did not happen) and that the 'present Oath of Allegiance could not be subscribed to'. The 'present oath' was to be changed on the afternoon of 5 December. The proposed oath of 'true faith *and allegiance*' was then confined to the new Irish Constitution, with faithfulness alone required in the case of the King – and the King no longer described as 'the Head of the State'. Also, as regards Ireland's dominion status, the word 'Empire' within the oath was replaced by the less offensive 'British Commonwealth of Nations' (Irish National Archives DE/2/304/5/6). All three decisions were made during the period that not only Duggan and Gavan Duffy but also Erskine Childers and Kevin O'Higgins were let in to join Cabinet ministers at the meeting.

Ministers Austin Stack and Cathal Brugha were, in general, hostile to any settlement that fell short of everything to which they had aspired in the War of Independence. Barton and Gavan Duffy thought that the British were bluffing to some extent and that further concessions might be won. Collins tended to agree with Griffith and Duggan that they had got the best terms possible. Childers was clearly opposed to aspects of the proposed settlement. The divisions were sharp – and unhelpful to Griffith, who had requested the meeting. Michael Collins was to tell the Dáil a fortnight later, 'It was well understood at the Cabinet Meeting that Sir James Craig was receiving a reply from the British Premier on Tuesday morning. Some conclusion as between the British Delegation and ourselves had, therefore, to be come to and handed in to the British Delegation on the Monday night.'

At one point the official note of the meeting includes this statement, 'Mr. Griffith to inform Mr. Lloyd George that the document could not be signed, to state that it is now a matter for the Dáil, and to try and put the blame on Ulster.' It is by no means clear from the note overall that this was a binding instruction to break off immediately, and it is neither specified to be a decision of the Cabinet nor said who made the statement or supported it. The hardline Minister for Defence, Cathal Brugha, reportedly claimed later that Griffith that day also explicitly promised not to sign 'the document' in London, and de Valera also spoke later of an 'express undertaking' by Griffith. Whether or not Griffith made such an explicit promise, unrecorded in the official notes, 'the document' on the table in Dublin was subsequently amended during negotiations and was not the one eventually signed in London. Moreover, as Barton told the Dáil on 19 December, Griffith tried repeatedly to persuade the British to agree to his returning to Dublin with that amended text rather than insisting on the Irish signing or rejecting it on the night of 5–6 December. In any event, signed or unsigned, the ultimate decision still lay with Dáil Éireann.

Ó Murchadha's notes refer to one particularly contentious exchange. Brugha, who had chosen not to go to London as a delegate, demanded to know more about the splitting of the delegation for various meetings there. He claimed that 'the British Government selected its men'. However, the Cabinet heard that while the British government was responsible for the arrangement (and Barton and Gavan Duffy had been uneasy about it), 'it had the approval of the whole delegation.' Griffith reassured the Cabinet that Dáil Éireann would have the final say.

The delegates left the Cabinet meeting in Dublin on Saturday without a precise brief; as Michael Collins was to tell the Dáil on 19 December, they took away 'impressions' rather than 'conclusions'. There was not even time for tea, as Collins complained later to Kitty Kiernan. He did manage to have the letter he had started in Downing Street the previous day finished and posted to her, scribbling on it, 'We were 8½ hours crossing. Ran down a boat and had to put back. Killed three men.' The delegates went from the meeting to board boats back to Britain. De Valera left Dublin to return to the West, rather than staying in the city to be continuously available for communication with his ministers at this time of crisis. 'Confused and inconclusive discussion in Irish Cabinet', recorded the promptly and well-informed British Cabinet secretary in his diary for that very day. It is suspected that British intelligence had an informant on the Irish side, perhaps a relative of a participant, but this has never been confirmed.

'Next day in London', wrote Pakenham in 1935, 'it was found impossible to achieve agreed recollection of what had been decided.' Tiredness alone was taking its toll. They knew that de Valera wanted them to make demands of the British again that had been well aired at the outset of negotiations – particularly for a level of independence from Crown and Empire that had been consistently rejected by Lloyd George. Michael Collins was fed up.

Breakdown, 4 December

In London on Sunday, 4 December, after an overnight journey by boat and train back from the previous day's cantankerous Cabinet meeting in Dublin, delegates faced into a demoralising day. Lloyd George wanted to see them that afternoon. Collins refused to attend the meeting, fully aware that they had been asked by de Valera to go back in to restate what would sound like the original Irish starting position. Griffith himself was reluctant to do so, but as chairman he dutifully went with Gavan Duffy and Barton.

Barton was to tell the Bureau of Military History in 1954, 'There was a difference of opinion between us as to what the British would agree to, and Collins objected to our going back again with proposals which he claimed the British had already turned down. Gavan Duffy and I thought more could be gained if we pressed further. Griffith agreed to accompany us, but Collins refused. Duggan also refused. Whatever Collins decided, Duggan always agreed with. Failure was foredoomed. To succeed, our case would have to have been pressed with vigour by all five of us.' One wonders why he went, then. In any event, it seems unlikely that even the presence of the entire Irish Cabinet that day would have changed Lloyd George's mind.

The meeting that Collins missed truly did not go well, with Gavan Duffy giving the British an excuse to break off negotiations on the matter of Ireland refusing to remain in the Empire, thus allowing the British to avoid a breakdown on the question of Northern Ireland's status and boundaries. The British felt that breaking on Ulster would look much worse internationally, and be harder to justify to their own voters, than breaking because Ireland was unwilling to be a member of the Empire.

Later that Sunday Griffith wrote to de Valera, 'They [the British] asked what was the difficulty about going in like Canada in the Empire? Gavan Duffy said that we should be as closely associated with them as the Dominions [such as Canada] in the large matters, and more so in the matter of defence but our difficulty is coming within the Empire. They jumped up at this and conversation came to a close, we undertaking to send them copies of our proposals tomorrow and they undertaking to send in a formal rejection tomorrow. They would, they said, inform Craig tomorrow that the negotiations were broken down. We then parted.'

Fifteen days later Barton was to tell Dáil Éireann, 'On Sunday, December 4th, the Conference had precipitately and definitely broken down.' Gavan Duffy informed deputies, 'On the 4th of December a sub-conference was held between the two sides at which Lloyd George broke with us on the Empire and broke definitely, subject to confirmation by his Cabinet the next morning. It might have been, or it might not have been, bluff.' When their fellow delegate Éamonn Duggan rose in the Dáil, he sounded annoyed, 'We came to a Cabinet meeting on a Saturday. We spent a whole day at it; in fact it was scarcely finished when we had to rush away to catch the boat back. We put up the proposals that the Cabinet said we should put up. They were turned down, and had been, two or three times previously. We told the Cabinet they would be turned down, but we carried out their instructions.'

Writing to de Valera from Hans Place on 4 December, within hours of the meeting breaking up, Griffith informed him that at five o'clock Barton, Duffy and himself had met Lloyd George, Chamberlain, Horne and Birkenhead at Downing Street. Griffith reminded the British that he had earlier given them assurances, and told them that Craig should now write them a letter accepting the essential unity of Ireland, 'I was seeking here if the break was to come making it come on Ulster rather than the Crown. They said Craig would not write such a letter, for he was going to refuse the proposals but they would nevertheless go ahead with the Treaty.' Griffith also informed de Valera that Lloyd George had said the amendments were 'a complete going back upon the discussions of the last week'. Lloyd George claimed, 'The amendments constituted a refusal to enter the Empire and accept the common bond of the Crown. They were but the same proposals which had already been discussed and rejected.'

Griffith put a brave face on things for de Valera, 'I pointed out there was a distinct effort to meet them in the proposals and instanced the oath which brought in the name of the King. A discussion followed. Mr. Barton argued that a permanent peace based on goodwill was what was needed, and what was offered by us. Mr. Gavan Duffy argued that for all purposes essential to them the proposals provided the necessary connection. I tried to work back on Ulster. They were asking us to give up our best ground without even a guarantee that Craig would accept the unity of the Irish Nation. There was nothing tangible in our hand. How could Ireland trust the faith of the British Government, etc?' Griffith wrote of the British having stated that if the Irish signed an agreement, they, the British, would immediately convene parliament to ratify it and 'hand us over Dublin Castle and withdraw their troops from the country'. He reported the British declaring that their dominions would denounce them if they even considered accepting the full Irish proposals. No English government could entertain them, they had said. 'I worked on Ulster again but could not get it into its proper place. They talked of their difficulties. We said we had just as many. We had tried to meet them.'

The meeting had taken a turn for the worse, with the British ending it when Gavan Duffy reasserted Ireland's unwillingness to be a member of the Commonwealth within the Empire. He had given them their chance to break.

Collins Fed Up, 4–5 December

Collins explained his absence from the meeting with Lloyd George on Sunday, 4 December as being 'for the reason that I had in my own estimation argued fully all points'. The British Cabinet secretary thought bluntly that Collins was 'fed up' with the muddle. Alone in his room at Cadogan Gardens, the Irishman wrote to Kitty Kiernan in Ireland, 'I dislike this place intensely on a Sunday; everything so quiet, and still, and so drearily dull. The outlook now is not inviting – through smoky, grimy windows, to a drab Square. Very, very unpleasant indeed – different from our own places, but then there's a job to be done, and for the moment here is the place. And that's that.'

Griffith must have been tired after his overnight journey from Dublin and the fruitless session with Lloyd George, but he did not go to bed early that Sunday. Instead, he sought a means of involving Collins again. He arranged to meet Thomas Jones, the British Cabinet secretary. At half past one on Monday morning, after they had parted, Jones wrote in his diary, 'I saw Arthur Griffith at midnight for an hour alone. He was labouring under a deep sense of the crisis and spoke throughout with the greatest earnestness and unusual emotion. One was bound to feel that to break with him would be infinitely tragic.' Griffith is said to have described the meeting to Jones as 'our first attempt at secret diplomacy'. He tried to impress on Jones the need for concessions to convince the Dáil. Jones agreed to a request from Griffith that Lloyd George would meet Michael Collins a few hours later to 'have a heart-to-heart talk with him'. And so, as Jones put it, 'Arthur Griffith went over at 1.00 [a.m.] to hunt out Collins to fix this up.'

A correspondent for Monday morning's *Freeman's Journal* in Dublin spoke of 'an air of gloom' in London, 'Journalists who have been accustomed to visit Downing Street almost daily for years past informed me that they never remember seeing so much depression within the portals of No. 10 as prevailed last night.' Nevertheless, following Griffith's intervention, Collins and Lloyd George met alone at half past nine on Monday morning. In his memorandum of their encounter, Collins reported that the prime minister began by indicating that he was having a meeting of his Cabinet at noon and was putting it to them that the conference had broken as a result of the session with Griffith, Barton and Gavan Duffy the previous afternoon, 'I said I understood that. He went on to say that the break was therefore definitely on the question of "within or without" the Empire (at this stage he did not refer to allegiance except to say that he would be willing to consider any form of Oath in order to meet or attempt to meet our wishes).'

Collins tried to focus the meeting on Ulster – 'the North-East', as he called it. The prime minister remarked how Collins himself had pointed out on a previous occasion that Northern Ireland would be forced economically to come into a united Ireland by circumstances prevailing once the Treaty proposals were accepted, 'I assented [had Lloyd George actually endorsed his previous point?] but I said the position was so serious owing to certain recent actions that for my part I was anxious to secure a definite reply from Craig and his colleagues, and that I was as agreeable to a reply rejecting as accepting [the proposition that Northern Ireland would be part of a united Ireland with its own institutions].' Collins reported telling Lloyd George that if Northern Ireland opted to remain in the United Kingdom, then the Irish Free State 'would save Tyrone and Fermanagh, parts of Derry, Armagh and Down by a boundary commission, and thus avoid such things as the [recent] raid on the Tyrone County Council and the ejection of the staff.' Collins added that 'Another such incident would, in my view, inevitably lead to a conflict, and this conflict in the nature of things (assuming for instance that some of the Anglo-Northern police were killed or wounded) would inevitably rapidly spread throughout Ireland.'

Collins and Lloyd George also discussed the oath of allegiance to the Crown which the British were then demanding that deputies in Dáil Éireann would take, as well as the matter of defence and the British use of Irish ports, 'Mr. Lloyd George said that if I had the idea of building submarines they could not allow that. I said my objection was on the principle that we could build nothing.' There was clearly scope for some compromise here.

Before Lloyd George left to brief the King on developments, he and Collins agreed that there might be a meeting of both sides at two o'clock that day. That meeting in fact took place.

Shortly before it did, the British Cabinet assembled and was told that 'the division of opinion which had manifested itself among the Irish Representatives in London, also existed in the Irish Cabinet' (UK National Archives CAB 23/27/16. p. 215).

An 'Ultimatum', 5–6 December

Neither the Irish nor the British were happy when they met at three o'clock on the afternoon of Monday, 5 December, for what transpired to be the crucial final talks. These would go on past midnight. Yet it was not a full session of all delegates on each side, just a scheduled sub-conference attended only by Griffith, Collins and Barton on the Irish side, and Lloyd George, Chamberlain, Birkenhead and (for part of the time) Churchill on the British.

The Irish were tired after weeks of wrangling, a dash to Dublin on Friday and Saturday, the breaking off of talks by Lloyd George on Sunday and overnight efforts to get Michael Collins back on board. The British were impatient. Writing in his *World Crisis: The Aftermath* (Thornton Butterworth, 1929), Winston Churchill described the mood, 'In the end, after two months of futilities and rigmarole, scarred by outrages in Ireland in breach of the truce, unutterably wearied Ministers faced the Irish Delegates, themselves in actual desperation and knowing well that death stood at their elbows.' British officials briefed the press that the situation was 'most critical'.

Griffith's note of the meeting begins, 'Things were so strenuous and exhausting that the sequence of conversation is not in many cases clear in my mind today [...] The Conference opened with the British Delegates in a bad mood. They had a full Cabinet meeting previously and apparently had had a rough time.' Barton's note informed de Valera that Lloyd George soon got excited, 'He shook his papers in the air, declared that we were trying deliberately to bring about a break on Ulster because our people in Ireland had refused to come within the Empire and that Arthur Griffith was letting him down where he had promised not to do so.'

Lloyd George's opening gambit was to declare that he must know once and for all exactly where the Irish stood as regards the Ulster proposals. He claimed that the Ulster proposals which the British had sent to the Irish in a draft agreement the previous week, and which had been discussed on Saturday in Dublin, 'were exactly those to which Arthur Griffith had agreed and on which he had undertaken not to let him down'. This seems to have been a reference to the Boundary Commission idea. According to Barton, Griffith replied 'that he had not let him down and did not intend to do so, but that before he gave a decision on the earlier articles in the document he must have a reply from Craig either accepting or refusing the unity of Ireland.' Both Chamberlain and Lloyd George, wrote Barton, argued strongly that such a proposition was 'inadmissible, unreasonable and contrary to the undertaking not to let Lloyd George down'. Chamberlain claimed that 'it was due to the confidence they had in our undertaking that they would not be let down by us that his colleagues and he had adopted the attitude they did [...] and staked thereon their political future.'

However, Griffith's official 'personal assurances' from 2 November – sent to Lloyd George with the knowledge of other delegates and of de Valera – and his undertaking of 12 November – not to dismiss the Boundary Commission idea before Craig replied – had all been (as seen above) conditional and not absolute. Lloyd George never did secure the response from Craig that Griffith had sought, and the failure to make Northern Ireland party to the Boundary Commission proposal was ultimately one of the reasons why that body failed.

As the session continued on 5 December, the British assailed the Irish with references to assurances by Griffith, without Barton recording – or perhaps knowing – what exactly were the specific assurances, if any, that they had in mind. In the absence of clarity, and given what was about to happen at the meeting, the British delegates appear to have been intent on overwhelming the Irish. Churchill, who had been (in the words of the UK Cabinet secretary's diary) 'breathing fire and slaughter' about Ireland at a meeting of the British Cabinet in Scotland in September, said now that he would oppose Ireland having a navy of its own.

There was a pause in proceedings. The Irish decided amongst themselves to back Griffith's insistence on a response from Craig. When the meeting resumed, it seemed at first to be calmer. Churchill toned down his rhetoric and agreed that Ireland might have some vessels of its own for coastal defence. Griffith too gave something, but it was not much. He said that he personally would dispense with a reply from Craig but that his colleagues were in a different position and had not been involved in the November discussion with Lloyd George about the proposal

– that 'it was not fair to demand acceptance or refusal from them before Craig replied.' This was a common negotiating ploy, sounding flexible while regretting that you had to convince colleagues who needed more concessions to be persuaded.

Lloyd George did not respond kindly. The prime minister now delivered his infamous ultimatum. According to Barton, Lloyd George said 'he had always taken it that Arthur Griffith spoke for the Delegation.' The prime minister argued that 'we were all plenipotentiaries and that it was now a matter of peace or war and we must each of us make up our minds. He required that every delegate should sign the document and recommend it, or there was no agreement. He said that they as a body had hazarded their political future and we must do likewise and take the same risks.' Lloyd George looked at Barton, as the latter noted, 'At one time he particularly addressed himself to me and said very solemnly that those who were not for peace must take full responsibility for the war that would immediately follow refusal by any Delegate to sign the Articles of Agreement.'

The prime minister produced two letters, one of which he said would go that night to Craig in Belfast. The first was a cover letter to accompany the proposals for a treaty; it stated that the Irish delegation had agreed to recommend the proposals for acceptance by Dáil Éireann. The second noted that the Irish delegation had failed to come to an agreement and therefore he had no proposals to send to Craig. Lloyd George 'stated that he would have to have our agreement or refusal to the proposals by 10 p.m. that evening. That a special train and destroyer were ready to carry either one letter or the other to Belfast and that he would give us until ten o'clock to decide.'

Austen Chamberlain's account of the meeting, at which he too sat, is blunter. Writing his memoir *Down the Years* more than a decade later, but ostensibly quoting Lloyd George's words, he recalled the prime minister saying that the second letter for Craig meant 'the Sinn Féin representatives refuse the oath of allegiance and refuse to come within the Empire.' Chamberlain added that Lloyd George addressed the Irish directly, 'If I send this letter, it is war – and war within three days! Which letter am I to send?' The prime minister called on them to think again before they rejected 'so generous a settlement'.

In Churchill's version of 1929, the prime minister 'stated bluntly that we could concede no more and debate no further. They must settle now; they must sign the agreement for a Treaty in the form to which after all these weeks it had attained, or else quit; and further, that both sides would be free to resume whatever warfare they could wage against each other. This was an ultimatum delivered, not through diplomatic channels, but face to face, and all present knew and understood that nothing else was possible.' He added, 'The Irishmen gulped down the ultimatum phlegmatically.'

According to Churchill, 'Mr Griffith said, speaking in his soft voice and with his modest manner, "I will give the answer of the Irish Delegates at nine to-night; but, Mr. Prime Minister, I personally will sign this agreement and will recommend it to my countrymen". "Do I understand, Mr. Griffith," said Mr. Lloyd George, "that though everyone else refuses you will nevertheless agree to sign?" "Yes, that is so, Mr. Prime Minister," replied this quiet little man of great heart and of great purpose. Michael Collins rose looking as if he was going to shoot someone, preferably himself. In all my life I have never seen so much passion and suffering in restraint.' As the Irish got into their cars to return to Hans Place, reporters asked Collins if they would return. 'I don't know,' he replied.

Churchill recalled that he and the other British 'then went off and drummed our heels and had some food and smoked, and discussed plans of campaign. No one expected that anyone but Mr. Griffith would agree, and what validity would his solitary signature possess? As for ourselves, we had already ruptured the loyalties of our friends and supporters.'

The Agreement Signed

The British had issued their ultimatum, and the Irish, unhappy back at Hans Place, decided to sign the agreement. 'Why', asks Pakenham in his *Peace by Ordeal* (1935), 'was no use made of the telephone to Dublin?' Nicholas Mansergh, in *The Unresolved Question* (Yale, 1991), provides an answer, 'Who was to be telephoned? The President? He [...] at the vital time appears to have been in Ennis [Co. Clare]. Stack was in Dublin but telephone conversation between Griffith and Stack was as likely to result in discord as accord. There was also the near certainty that the line would have been tapped [if, indeed, the connection even held up].' De Valera had made no arrangement to be available for consultation.

At 11.20 p.m. on Monday, 5 December, the Irish returned to Downing Street for some further discussion about the final terms. Churchill described the delegates as 'superficially calm and very quiet' when they entered the room where the British waited. Griffith's insistence that Craig should be obliged to accept either a united Ireland or a redrawn border had been brushed aside by the British. Barton's note of the next three hours is just four hundred and twenty words long. Its last lines are laden with the weight of history, 'Lloyd George then asked whether we as a Delegation were prepared to accept these Articles of Agreement and to stand by them in our Parliament as they as a Delegation would stand by them in theirs. Arthur Griffith replied "We do".' Churchill wrote that 'There was a long pause, or there seemed to be', between Lloyd George's question and Griffith's answer – which Churchill gives in a longer form, 'Then Mr. Griffith said, "Mr. Prime Minister, the Delegation is willing to sign the agreements, but there are a few points of drafting which perhaps it would be convenient if I mentioned at once".' Churchill thought that 'Thus, by the easiest of gestures, he carried the whole matter into the region of minor detail, and everyone concentrated upon these points with overstrained interest so as to drive the main issue into the background for ever. Soon we were talking busily about technicalities and verbal corrections, and holding firmly to all these lest worse should befall.'

The two sides, while awaiting copies of the final agreed draft, discussed procedural matters and the future release of thousands of Irish political prisoners. The draft was then read, agreed to and signed. It appears that no photograph was taken of the momentous signing. Barton wrote next day, 'The British delegation lined up to shake hands and say good-bye, and the Conference ended at 2.20 a.m. on December 6th.'

'As the Irishmen rose to leave', wrote Churchill, 'the British Ministers upon a strong impulse walked round and for the first time shook hands.'

At a Cabinet meeting in Dublin three days later, Griffith would be recorded as saying, 'If I could have left it to [the] Dáil,

[I] would have. No choice. Letters going [to Craig;] we took decision and don't regret it.'

Among the support team waiting in Hans Place for the Irish to return was Griffith's personal secretary, Kathleen McKenna. Recalling that night fifty years later for the *Capuchin Annual*, she wrote that the light in the hall was dim when cars arrived at about a quarter to three. She ran to the door as Diarmuid O'Hegarty entered, 'the Treaty document rolled round like a scroll in his hands'. He unrolled it for those waiting to see it. They were 'gazing, astonished or incredulous as to its import'. Barton later told the Bureau of Military History, 'The original document was brought to Hans Place next morning to be signed by Duggan and Gavan Duffy, but Duggan had already left for Dublin.' His signature was found elsewhere in the house at Hans Place; it was cut out and pasted onto the agreement for a treaty.

A quotation has been attributed to Michael Collins, and very often repeated, to the effect that when he signed the agreement that night, he signed his own death warrant. This statement cannot be confirmed, as only one biographer, Rex Taylor, has claimed to have seen the letter in which it was reportedly made. The name that Taylor gave for the businessman to whom it was ostensibly addressed appears to have been fictional, and the person has never been publicly identified (Deirdre McMahon, 'Michael Collins: his biographers Piaras Béaslaí and RexTaylor', in *Michael Collins and the Making of the Irish State*, ed. G. Doherty and D. Keogh [Cork, 1988], pp.133–5).

Collins did write to his friend Kitty Kiernan on 6 December to say that he had not got to bed until five o'clock that morning, adding, 'I don't know how things will go now but with God's help we have brought peace to this land of ours – a peace which will end this old strife of ours forever' (*In Great Haste*, ed. León Ó Broin).

As regards Griffith, his personal secretary Kathleen McKenna wrote, 'It is a grave untruth that has been deliberately repeated to assert that Arthur Griffith walked up and down the hall all night with his head in his hands, despairingly. In the first place there was only a small square of hall similar to a landing; and, secondly, Arthur Griffith was not a man to make a demonstration of his sentiments, no matter what they might be. I saw that he was stern, serious, determined, patient; neither joyful nor depressed. He had done what he had done because he was convinced in his soul that it was the right thing, and the only thing to do.'

Although he very reluctantly signed the agreement for a treaty on 6 December, Gavan Duffy was to tell the Dáil on 23 December, 'I do not think that […] it is an adequate motive for rejection to point out that some of us signed the Treaty under duress […] It is necessary before you reject the Treaty to go further than that and to produce to the people of Ireland a rational alternative. My heart is with those who are against the Treaty, but my reason is against them, because I can see no rational alternative.'

Minutes of a British Cabinet meeting held ten hours after the agreement was signed on 6 December indicate that Lloyd George and his ministers seemed elated at what they regarded as a triumph on their part. They 'generally agreed' that 'the rough treatment to which the Irish extremists had been subjected during the last twelve months […] had brought home to the men in the field the need for some equitable compromise' (UK National Archives, CAB 23/27/17). Both sides had to persuade sceptical colleagues that the Treaty represented success, and ministers in each government who had signed the agreement no doubt presented it in the best light. For the Irish there was a bonus in that thousands of nationalist internees were now to be released by the British – the possibility of them all spending Christmas 1921 imprisoned having been yet one more pressure on the plenipotentiaries.

De Valera was annoyed when he heard that the agreement had been signed without his final consent. Yet, later on the day of that signing, he donned academic robes in his capacity as Chancellor of the National University of Ireland and calmly chaired an evening event to mark the anniversary of Dante Alighieri's death in 1321. That Italian poet's vision of hell, his *Inferno*, warns of the consequences of anger, violence and treachery. Any such warnings were insufficient to prevent the optimism around both the truce of July 1921 and the opening of the Peace Conference in London from now evaporating in a slide towards civil war.

Mystery Solved

At the outset of peace talks in October 1921, the British encouraged Northern Ireland to become part of a proposed all-Ireland state within the Empire. In such circumstances, they said, Northern Ireland would retain a distinct local identity and a parliament within an internally partitioned Ireland.

Unionists were subsequently informed that if they insisted on remaining within the United Kingdom, the new border of Northern Ireland might have to be redrawn by a boundary commission.

During the first week of November 1921, Lionel Curtis, British secretary to the peace talks, hastily prepared a memorandum of fourteen pages to guide the British negotiators on a boundary commission proposal and other matters. Between 8 and 12 November, written corrections and marginal notes were added following discussions with the UK Cabinet secretary Thomas Jones and another official, Sir Edward Grigg. The memorandum was a draft, entitled 'Proposals to Ulster', and a copy of it – including those corrections and notes, and with its last page identified as being in a finalised typed form – is now archived in the library of the Houses of Parliament at Westminster (LG/F/181/4/1). All or some of its contents were also discussed that same week with some of the Irish plenipotentiaries who spoke with Lloyd George and his Cabinet secretary about the developing Boundary Commission idea (considered above).

Lloyd George used the finalised text on the last page of that Curtis memorandum on the last night of the peace talks, causing confusion then and subsequently. His way of using it has damaged Arthur Griffith's reputation. The text formalised the idea that a commission would be appointed to determine the precise border between Northern Ireland and the rest of Ireland in the event of Northern Ireland deciding not to become part of a new all-Ireland state. The origin of the text flourished by Lloyd George that night is now explained.

Thomas Pakenham, in his influential book *Peace by Ordeal* (1935), misunderstood its origin. He built a theory around it that was ostensibly based on a conversation he had with Austen Chamberlain more than a decade after the Treaty was agreed. In his book, Pakenham recalls that he spoke with Chamberlain 'in some detail' about various matters but that Chamberlain 'felt unable' to give him the use of his papers and simply 'read to me his contemporary notes of the crucial meetings'. Pakenham thought that Arthur Griffith had been duped by Chamberlain into assenting secretly to a proposition that implicitly accepted the already existing partition of Ireland as a basis for a treaty, and that this somehow compromised the entire Treaty process and predetermined its result. *Peace by Ordeal* is engagingly written and persuasive, and many subsequent writers have relied on it in respect to this matter. But Griffith was neither a dupe nor a knave, and made no such secret deal.

The wording of the document of two hundred typed words that Lloyd George flourished appears to have corresponded exactly to the last page of the fourteen in the Curtis memorandum as finalised. The same text had also been incorporated, in early November, into two drafts of a letter for Lloyd George to send in reply to Northern Ireland's premier, James Craig. On 11 November, Craig had ruled out absolutely an all-Ireland parliament. The British draft replies to him – A and B – are both marked 'secret' in the UK National Archives (CAB 43/2/4, ff. 142-5).

When Lloyd George had lunch with Griffith at Philip Sassoon's house on Saturday, 12 November, they discussed the letter that Lloyd George told Griffith he intended to send to Craig on Monday, 14 November – the letter that was intended to include the proposal for a boundary commission to delimit the area of Northern Ireland.

According to a handwritten note by Jones on the last page of Curtis's memo in the parliamentary archives, that page had been 'Retyped. Copy Shown A.G. Sunday 13.xi.21' (the day after Griffith had lunch with Lloyd George). Jones did not indicate that Griffith ('A.G.') had either signed a copy of it or assented to its contents on that day – something Jones would likely have done if that were the case. It is very unlikely that Griffith did so; it would have been contrary to his cautious personal style. It would also have been inconsistent with the evidence of his immediate responses to the British idea, detailed in his letters to de Valera and in Jones's diary (as quoted above in the section on the Boundary Commission, entitled 'Redrawing the Border').

If Ulster did not see her way to accept
immediately the principle of a Parliament of
All-Ireland - coupled with the retention by the
Parliament of Northern Ireland of the powers con-
ferred upon it by the Act of 1920 and such other
safeguards as have already been suggested in my letter
of 10th November - we should then propose to create
such Parliament for All-Ireland but to allow Ulster
the right within a specified time on an address to the
Throne carried in both Houses of the Ulster Parliament
to elect to remain subject to the Imperial Parliament
for all the reserved services.   In this case she
would continue to exercise through her own Parliament
all her present rights; she would continue to be
represented in the British Parliament and she would
continue subject to British taxation except in so far
as already modified by the Act of 1920. In this case
however it would be necessary to revise the boundary
of Northern Ireland.   This might be done by a Boundary
Commission which would be directed to adjust the line
both by inclusion and exclusion so as to make the
Boundary conform as closely as possible to the wishes
of the population.

Lionel Curtis, UK Secretary to Peace Conference, to Prime Minister Lloyd George, 'Proposals to Ulster', memorandum dated 8 November 1921, page 14. [Parliamentary Archives, Houses of Parliament, London, LG/F/181/4/1]. The note at the bottom of the page, handwritten by UK Cabinet Secretary Thomas Jones, reads 'Retyped. Copy Shown A.G. Sunday 13.xi.21.'

In any event, the text found on the last page of Curtis's memo and in the drafts of the letter to Craig was omitted from the actual letter sent to Craig two days after Griffith discussed it with Lloyd George on 12 November (Prime Minister to Craig, UK National Archives, CAB 43/2/4, ff. 147-9). On 15 November Griffith informed de Valera, 'The answer he sent Craig was not as he first arranged.' Griffith understood that the British were holding back the details of a boundary commission proposal until later, 'to put it up then as an "ultimatum" to Ulster'. The omission gives rise to a suspicion that the British were perhaps not as committed to the idea of a boundary commission as the Irish delegates were led to believe. Nevertheless, a definite British proposal for an open-ended boundary commission for Ulster was subsequently included in documents seen by all five Irish delegates, and also by their Cabinet colleagues in Dublin, in advance of the final night of Treaty negotiations on 5–6 December.

Pakenham does not support with evidence his suggestion that Griffith had somehow 'made startling and secret concessions' by giving 'assent' on 13 November to the content of the text found on the last page of the Curtis memo, which Pakenham thought Chamberlain and Jones had cunningly composed that day. However, his theory is so enmeshed in the plausible narrative of his *Peace by Ordeal* that it has even misled biographers of Griffith – including this author, on one occasion – into using the word 'assent' loosely in respect to Griffith's response to the Boundary Commission idea in early November.

Besides Chamberlain, another of Pakenham's principal sources was the plenipotentiary Robert Barton. Barton signed the agreement for the Treaty most reluctantly, and by the time he helped Pakenham with *Peace by Ordeal*, he was firmly in de Valera's camp. The historian Nicholas Mansergh has characterised Pakenham himself as 'sympathetic to de Valera's position'. Barton's and Pakenham's accounts need to be seen in this light.

As soon as the final session of the talks ended on 5–6 December, Griffith asked Barton to write up what had happened for de Valera. Barton's memorandum survives. It includes this:

> Lloyd George got excited. He shook his papers in the air, declared that we were trying deliberately to bring about a break on Ulster because our people in Ireland had refused to come within the Empire and that Arthur Griffith was letting him down where he had promised not to do so. He produced a paper from an envelope, stated that he had shown it to Arthur Griffith at [Philip Sassoon]'s house and that Arthur Griffith had agreed to its contents. Lloyd George referred to this document as a letter and thereby mystified me and appeared to mystify Michael Collins. I could not recollect the existence of any letter on this subject other than the one Arthur Griffith wrote to Lloyd George on November 2nd after consultation with the other members of the Delegation. The paper was then passed across the table. It proved to be a memorandum, not a letter, and read as follows:-

> *If Ulster did not see her way to accept immediately the principle of a Parliament of All-Ireland – coupled with the retention by the Parliament of Northern Ireland of the powers conferred upon it by the Act of 1920 and such other safeguards as have already been suggested in my letter of 10th November – we should then propose to create such Parliament for All-Ireland but to allow Ulster the right within a specified time on an address to the Throne carried in both houses of the Ulster Parliament*

> to elect to remain subject to the Imperial Parliament for all
> the reserved services. In this case she would continue to exercise
> through her own Parliament all her present rights; she would
> continue to be represented in the British Parliament and she
> would continue subject to British taxation except in so far as
> already modified by the Act of 1920. In this case, however, it
> would be necessary to revise the boundary of Northern Ireland.
> This might be done by a Boundary Commission which would
> be directed to adjust the line both by inclusion and exclusion so
> as to make the Boundary conform as closely as possible to the
> wishes of the population.

The present author has recently identified the words quoted by Barton above as being word-for-word the text on the last page of the Curtis memo – which Thomas Jones recorded as having been shown to Griffith in November, typed up. It is also virtually word-for-word (with a couple of insignificant minor changes) the text in the two draft letters for sending to Craig.

Barton's extant notes of that night (Irish National Archives DE/2/304/1/91) do not include the actual document itself that Lloyd George passed across the table. Presumably the prime minister referred to it as a 'letter' because he recalled it having been incorporated, before 12 November, into the drafts of his proposed letter to Craig. So why does Barton write that 'it proved to be a memorandum, not a letter'? How did he know that? He gives no identifying features, such as a memo writer's name or the name of a person to whom it was addressed, or a title or date such as one usually finds on a memo – and there are indeed no such details on the last page of the Curtis memo. Pakenham, in his book, simply reproduces verbatim Barton's transcription, providing no identifying features and no corroborating source. He attributes the memo to the cunning of his informant, Chamberlain, on 13 November.

Had Pakenham ever seen the original text produced by Lloyd George? In a letter published by the *Irish Times*, on 31 May 2021, Brian Maye – whose own biography of Griffith appeared in 1997 – recalled that 'When I was researching my book on Arthur Griffith back in the 1990s, I wrote to Frank Pakenham, by then Lord Longford, posing a number of questions. I was particularly interested in this "document" as I had been unable to find either it or where it was. I received a very courteous reply [from Pakenham], on House of Lords notepaper, in which some of my questions were answered but no reference was made to the document I couldn't locate.'

If Barton had identified the source of the original text produced by Lloyd George on the night of 5–6 December, the author of *Peace by Ordeal* might not have essayed a theory that impugned Griffith as some kind of dupe. Whether or not Lloyd George produced the text deliberately to confound the Irish at that last fraught session of talks, he clearly managed to confuse them. Yet the prime minister himself had been confused about the same page of the Curtis memorandum on 23 November. Then, his Cabinet secretary Thomas Jones wrote in his diary, 'he told me to produce at once the document I had shewn Arthur Griffith at the Grosvenor Hotel on Sunday, November 13th. When I produced it he said it was not the one, but luckily Chamberlain came to my support.'

The volume of Jones's published diary relating to Ireland has no record of a meeting with Griffith on 13 November. The long list of various Peace Conference meetings that Erskine Childers, the Irish delegation's principal secretary, submitted to Dáil Éireann in 1921 gives Jones as last meeting Griffith at the Grosvenor on Friday, 11 November (National Library of Ireland, MS 48,068/5). Indeed, Barton himself indicates in his notes of the meeting of 5–6 December that Lloyd George then asserted that Griffith had agreed to the contents on the last page of Curtis's memo when the two men met in Philip Sassoon's house. Even were it true that Griffith had personally agreed to the proposal then – and the evidence is that he did not do so; that he insisted it was just a British proposal – that meeting between the two men in Sassoon's house definitely happened on Saturday, 12 November. This was the day *before* the day on which – according to Pakenham – the same text was allegedly composed by Chamberlain and allegedly agreed secretly by Griffith.

Throughout, Griffith sought Craig's response to the Boundary Commission idea – as an alternative to the prospect of a united Ireland of any kind, which unionists found so unpalatable. He wanted to have this before asking his delegation to take a position on it. He had told de Valera in November that 'If the Ulstermen accepted it, we would have to discuss it with him [Lloyd George] in the privacy of the Conference.' He had promised Lloyd George that his team would not 'repudiate' the idea before Craig considered it, and had not let Lloyd George down in that respect. He was still seeking Craig's response on the night of 5 December. The British failed to elicit it for him. In his report to de Valera next day, Barton wrote that Griffith had told Lloyd George that it was not fair to demand acceptance or refusal from the Irish delegates before Craig answered. He added, 'Considerable discussion took place here on the justice and injustice of our being asked to agree or disagree before Craig replied, and Arthur Griffith made repeated efforts to avoid the question being put to Michael Collins and myself.'

The Anglo-Irish Treaty

On 7 January 1922 Dáil Éireann approved the Treaty. A short document of eighteen 'Articles', its full text is easily found online but the main points are outlined here.

It begins by declaring in Articles 1 and 2 that 'Ireland shall have the same constitutional status in the Community of Nations known as the British Empire as the Dominion of Canada, the Commonwealth of Australia, the Dominion of New Zealand, and the Union of South Africa, with a Parliament having powers to make laws for the peace, order and good government of Ireland and an Executive responsible to that Parliament, and shall be styled and known as the Irish Free State.' The dominions listed were independent, but they retained the British king or queen as their symbolical head of state within the Commonwealth. The Irish Free State was not a republic. In 1949 it would become one.

Article 3 provided that the representative of the Crown in Ireland was to be appointed in the same way as the Governor-General of Canada. During the 1930s, exercising what by then were legitimate dominion powers, Dáil Éireann replaced the office of governor-general with that of an elected president. The first was Douglas Hyde, who served from 1938 to 1945. The third was Éamon de Valera, from 1959 to 1973.

Article 4 set out the oath that all elected representatives in Dáil Éireann would now be required to swear. It included references to the Crown and Commonwealth, albeit in terms that Irish delegates had managed to have watered down in London on the afternoon of 5 December. In 1933 Dáil Éireann was to abolish that oath entirely. Nevertheless, given the oppressive role of British oaths in Irish political and religious history, its symbolism in 1921 was significant and divisive, and no Sinn Féin TD liked its wording, 'I do solemnly swear true faith and allegiance to the Constitution of the Irish Free State as by law established and that I will be faithful to H.M. King George V., his heirs and successors by law, in virtue of the common citizenship of Ireland with Great Britain and her adherence to and membership of the group of nations forming the British Commonwealth of Nations.' Griffith's strategy had been to try to extract maximum concessions on Northern Ireland from the British in return for some form of Irish association with the Crown through the Commonwealth. The self-governing dominions increasingly preferred the latter term to 'Empire', and H. Duncan Hall states in the *American Political Science Review*, 47/4 (1953) that it was used for the first time officially in this article of the Anglo-Irish Treaty. At the fraught last session on 5–6 December, the Irish delegates had had it substituted for the word 'Empire' in the draft of the oath in Article 4. When de Valera met Lloyd George in London in July 1921 for talks about talks, his spokesman had

had to deny reports that he then privately conceded that Ireland would remain in the British Commonwealth.

Under Article 5, the Irish Free State was to agree to pay a fair share of the United Kingdom's public debt at the time of independence, but the calculation of its contribution was to take into account past inequities in Ireland's financial treatment. The amount was to be settled by independent arbitration.

Until an arrangement could be made between the British and Irish governments whereby the Irish Free State would undertake its own coastal defence, Article 6 ensured that British forces were to undertake the defence by sea of Great Britain and Ireland. This was not intended to prevent the government of the Irish Free State from constructing or maintaining such vessels as were necessary for the protection of the revenue or the fisheries. The Irish Free State was also to allow Britain to use certain named harbours and other facilities; there was considerable resentment that the British would retain 'the Treaty ports' of Cobh (then 'Queenstown'), Berehaven and Lough Swilly. During the 1930s, however, the Irish government negotiated an ending of the arrangement.

The government of the Irish Free State agreed to pay fair compensation to judges, officials, policemen and other public servants who were discharged by it or who retired in consequence of the change of government not being to their liking. (The exception to this were the despised Auxiliaries and the Black and Tans.)

Under Article 12, Northern Ireland was given the right to opt out of the Irish Free State; if it did so, however, a boundary commission was to be set up 'consisting of three persons, one to be appointed by the Government of the Irish Free State, one to be appointed by the Government of Northern Ireland,

and one who shall be Chairman to be appointed by the British Government'. This Boundary Commission 'shall determine in accordance with the wishes of the inhabitants, so far as may be compatible with economic and geographic conditions, the boundaries between Northern Ireland and the rest of Ireland'. Both Griffith and Collins thought that this provision would result in swathes of Northern Ireland joining the Irish Free State. After their deaths in 1922, no change in the line of the border was ever made.

Potential problems for religious minorities in a divided Ireland were foreseen and addressed by Article 16, although how effectively so is a matter of opinion, 'Neither the Parliament of the Irish Free State nor the Parliament of Northern Ireland shall make any law so as either directly or indirectly to endow any religion or prohibit or restrict the free exercise thereof or give any preference or impose any disability on account of religious belief or religious status or affect prejudicially the right of any child to attend a school receiving public money without attending the religious instruction at the school or make any discrimination as respects State aid between schools under the management of different religious denominations or divert from any religious denomination or any educational institution any of its property except for public utility purposes and on payment of compensation.'

Majority Rule: 7 January 1922

Before the plenipotentiaries left for London, de Valera admitted that there was likely to be a disagreement in the Irish Cabinet about any final deal that they brought home. He said in Dáil Éireann on 23 August 1921, 'It is obvious that whenever there are negotiations, unless you are able to dictate terms you will have differences. Therefore it is obvious you will have sharp differences.'

He made a promise that same day, 'The Ministry [Cabinet] itself may not be able to agree and in such a case the majority would rule. Those who would disagree with me would resign.' He obviously did not foresee that those who were to 'disagree with me' would constitute the majority.

He continued, 'But I am looking at the worst possible thing that could happen, that if the plenipotentiaries go to negotiate a treaty or a peace, seeing that we are not in the position that we can dictate the terms, we will, therefore, have proposals brought back which cannot satisfy everybody, and will not, and my position is that when such a time comes I will be in a position, having discussed the matter with the Cabinet, to come forward with such proposals as we think wise and right. It will be then for you either to accept the recommendations of the Ministry or reject them. If you reject them you then elect a new Ministry. You would then be creating a definite active opposition.' He said that he was keeping his own mind 'in a fluid state'.

When the seven ministers of the Dáil Cabinet met in Dublin on 8 December to discuss the signed agreement, the future first 'President of the Executive' (prime minister) of the Irish Free State, W.T. Cosgrave, voted with Griffith, Collins and Barton to recommend the proposed Treaty to the Dáil, notwithstanding any reservations that the four men had. De Valera sided with the more militant Cathal Brugha and Austin Stack against doing so. Dáil Éireann then debated the agreement between 14 December and 7 January, holding some discussions behind closed doors.

On 16 December 1921 in London, the Anglo-Irish Treaty agreement was ratified by members of the House of Commons (401 votes to 58) and by members of the House of Lords (166 votes to 47). When the Dáil, on 7 January 1922, ratified it by 64 votes to 57, de Valera resigned as president and Griffith was elected to replace him in that role. A new Cabinet was appointed.

De Valera then became part of 'a definite active opposition', but presumably not the kind of opposition that he himself had foreseen when he used that term months earlier to describe the fate of those who would reject an agreement recommended to the Dáil by his Cabinet. His opposition, and that of Brugha and Stack, did not remain parliamentary. By March 1922 the *Cork Examiner* and *Freeman's Journal* were among newspapers reporting that he was warning voters that if they chose pro-Treaty candidates in the forthcoming general election, anti-Treaty forces would have to 'wade through Irish blood', and 'perhaps through that of some of the members of the Irish Government'. It was not only Lloyd George who could threaten the Irish government with war. In the general election of 16 June 1922, however, voters returned a significant pro-Treaty majority.

During the Civil War that followed, Arthur Griffith collapsed and died. Michael Collins was killed in an ambush. Cathal Brugha seems to have chosen to die; instead of slipping away or surrendering, he exited the besieged Hammam Hotel with a revolver in hand. Free State soldiers shot him. De Valera had earlier left the same hotel, and later resumed constitutional politics. In 1926 he founded the Fianna Fáil party, its members, after all, willing to take the Treaty's oath of faithfulness to the Crown in order to sit in Dáil Éireann. In due course, he was to become head of government and then head of state. Robert Barton came to support Fianna Fáil. Austin Stack, who did not do so, died in 1929. Gavan Duffy failed to be elected to the Dáil as an independent candidate in 1923, and thereafter pursued his career in law. The seventh member of the Cabinet that was in office during the Treaty negotiations in 1921 was W.T. Cosgrave. He became the first prime minister of the Irish Free State (an office known then as 'president' and later as 'Taoiseach').

For the principals in England, too, there were consequences, albeit political rather than mortal. Lloyd George and Chamberlain soon lost office. Churchill later wrote that 'The event was fatal to the Prime Minister. Within a year he had been driven from power. Many other causes, some at least of which could have been avoided, contributed to his fall; but the Irish Treaty and its circumstances were unforgivable by the most tenacious elements in the Conservative Party. Even among those who steadfastly supported it there were many who said, "It must needs be that offences come, but woe to that man by whom the offence cometh."' Churchill's biblical quotation (Matthew 18:7) was apt not just in respect to those on the British side who signed the agreement for a treaty.

The partitioning of Ireland by means of the United Kingdom Government of Ireland Act 1920 was undone neither by the War of Independence nor by the Treaty. Nonetheless, the Irish Free State did become a stepping-stone to greater independence, as Collins and Griffith had hoped it would when they decided to sign the agreement for a treaty on 6 December 1921. On 1 July 1937 the state's voters approved, in a plebiscite, de Valera's proposed new Constitution of Ireland. In 1949 an Irish government declared the Irish Free State to be a republic. The Republic of Ireland's defence forces have played an active role for the United Nations in keeping peace abroad, and Ireland is currently an elected member of the UN Security Council. The Irish state remains militarily neutral while being, at the same time, a full member of the European Union.

***

By the Same Author

Kenmare: History and Survival – Fr John O'Sullivan and the Famine Poor (2021)

The Enigma of Arthur Griffith: 'Father of Us All' (2020)

An Irish-American Odyssey: The Remarkable Rise of the O'Shaughnessy Brothers (2014)

The Power of Silence: Silent Communication in Daily Life (2011)

Irish Patriot, Publisher and Advertising Agent: Kevin J. Kenny (2011)

Moments That Changed Us: Ireland 1973–2005 (2005)

Fearing Sellafield (2003)

Battle of the Books: Cultural Controversy at a Dublin Library (2002)

The Role of Believing Communities in Building Peace in Ireland (1998)

Molaise: Abbot of Leighlin and Hermit of Holy Island (1998)

Tristram Kennedy and the Revival of Irish Legal Training (1996)

Kilmainham: A Settlement Older than Dublin (1995)

Standing on Bray Head: Hoping it Might Be So (poetry) (1995)

King's Inns and the Kingdom of Ireland, 1541–1800 (1992)